Urban Japanese Housewives

STUDIES OF THE EAST ASIAN INSTITUTE
COLUMBIA UNIVERSITY

Urban Japanese Housewives

At Home and in the Community

ANNE E. IMAMURA

University of Hawaii Press   *Honolulu*

97 96 95 94 93 92   5 4 3 2 1

Studies of the East Asian Institute, Columbia University
The East Asian Institute is Columbia University's center for
research, publication, and teaching on modern East Asia.
The Studies of the East Asian Institute were inaugurated in
1962 to bring to a wider public the significant new research
on modern and contemporary East Asia.

Library of Congress Cataloging-in-Publication Data
Imamura, Anne E., 1946–
  Urban Japanese housewives.

  (Studies of the East Asian Institute, Columbia
University)
  Bibliography: p.
  Includes index.
    1. Urban women—Japan. 2. Housewives—Japan.
  3. City and town life—Japan. I. Title. II. Series:
Studies of the East Asian Institute.
HQ1762.I468 1987   305.4'2'0952   86–27262
ISBN 0–8248–1082–1

ISBN 0–8248–1499–1 (pbk)

For my parents
Robert H. and Irene E. Sommers

Contents

Acknowledgments

The completion of a study such as this places the author in an enormous amount of debt—intellectual, professional, and personal. Most of it cannot even be acknowledged. Nevertheless, I would like first of all to acknowledge my great intellectual debt to Herbert Passin, my dissertation advisor for this study. I benefited immeasurably from his willingness to share his knowledge of Japanese society, to introduce me into networks in Japan, and to read draft after draft of my work. My debt to him is profound.

During my research in Japan, Professor Aoi Kazuo of the Sociology Department of the University of Tokyo not only showed infinite patience in dealing with one revised questionnaire after another (and my handwritten Japanese) but also went to great pains to help me gain entry into my research site. The staff of the local city office and the community center who so graciously gave their time and energy to answer my questions and make certain I was getting a well-rounded picture of the local situation deserve more credit than I can express. The women who allowed me to share their coffee hours and recreation time, those who allowed me to interview them in their homes, and those who cooperated with the survey deserve more appreciation than space allows.

Among the many who so generously gave of their time and experience I owe special thanks to George Akita, Gary Allinson, Robert E. Cole, Hara Kimi, Iwao Sumiko, Eugene Litwak, James W. Morley, and James White. The finished product owes much to the editorial pencil of Anita O'Brien, the word-processing consultation of Geraldine Todd, and the long hours of typing by Marcia Karth and Joyce Sterling. The research would not have been possible without the generous funding of the Japan Foundation and the Fulbright-Hays Doctoral Dissertation Research Abroad Program.

There is also a nonprofessional requirement for producing a study such as this: the personal support of one's family. In this regard, I wish to express my gratitude for the support and encouragement of my parents, Robert H. and Irene Sommers, and my husband, Katsuyuki, who have put up with many inconveniences over the years for my sake. A special kind of appreciation goes to my son, Haruto Robert, whose birth was a happy addition to but not an interruption of this research, and to my daughter, Alysia Julia, who joined us between first draft and final. The responsibility for the content, of course, is entirely my own.

1 Introduction

In many ways my choice of topic for this study was a selfish one. Gerald Curtis advised Susan Pharr that "researchers owe it to themselves to study those topics that they find personally interesting as well as intellectually engaging." (See Pharr 1981, xiii–xiv.) In the same spirit, this topic developed out of several years of unsatisfied curiosity fed by personal experience and the inability to find in the literature sufficient answers to the questions I raise here.

My curiosity began in 1970. Living in a small apartment building in a Tokyo suburb, I looked out on a public housing project, a *danchi*.[1] Day after day I observed the men taking the same commuter trains as I and returning late—9, 10, 11 P.M., or later—often at least a bit tipsy. On weekends I noted that either the men went out alone, often carrying golf bags, or the men and their children would set off on the train without the women, apparently to a park or amusement center. It was obvious that the apartments were small, and a family of four was typically living in what is called a 2DK: two rooms (one 6-mat room and one 4.5-mat room)[2] and a dining kitchen. What, I wondered, did the women do? I could see them standing on stairwells, observing children at play and gossiping. I could also see them making regular daily trips to the food shops at about 4 P.M. But only occasionally did I see them leaving as families on the weekends, and my friends and my landlord indicated that parents seldom leave children with sitters so they can go out together or for couples to visit back and forth casually. Rather, men had their own business and social lives outside the family and (with the exception of shopkeepers) outside the neighborhood. Occasionally the husband would be prevailed upon for "Sunday service"— taking care of the children so the mother could go shopping in a department store or perhaps attend an annual class gathering.

1

None of my observations fit in with my own Midwestern American images of family life. Furthermore, I knew that keeping such a small apartment clean could not occupy a woman's entire day and that, especially after the children were in school, the housewives must have many hours to fill. What, I wondered, did they do all day?

I myself was newly married and for the first time becoming involved in my Japanese husband's family, shopkeepers in a small town on the island of Hokkaido. Visiting my in-laws as a family member showed me the differences in life-styles between my family and their neighbors and the *danchi* families I was seeing in Tokyo. Because shops in the Hokkaido town are run by families, fathers and husbands are present and visible to their families. Moreover, families tend to stay in the small town for years or even generations, and both men and women know one another. During lulls in business they visit one another's homes for tea. Since these women not only run their homes and raise more children than the *danchi* women but also work as hard as their husbands in the family business and yet still find time to visit with one another, the *danchi* woman must have even more time on her hands than I originally thought. I realized that the questions I had been asking were not limited to *danchi* wives but applied to all urban wives who were not engaged in the family business or similar work. What did they do all day, and with whom did they do it?

The literature on contemporary urban Japanese society tells much about the salary man. (See, for example, Dore 1958 and Vogel 1967.) The company has taken over many functions of the extended family and the village, and the neighborhood plays less and less a role in his economic well-being. He has little time or interest in neighborhood affairs; rather, his involvement, business and social, is primarily with workmates or school friends, carried on outside the home, which separates him from the family. The literature also points out that as the economic importance of the neighborhood declines, the family abandons much of the traditional visiting and gift giving that have strengthened cooperative ties in the past. Rather, concern is focused inward toward the family itself. Only the formalities of introducing oneself when moving into a neighborhood are maintained, so that in emergencies the family might ask their neighbors for assistance. Increasing expectations that children will go on to higher education, as well as the difficulties of the university examination system, concentrate a great deal of the mother's time and energy on the education of her children. The term "education mother" was coined to describe the woman who pushes her children ahead at all costs, constantly helping them with homework and often placing them in *juku* (private prep schools) after regular school hours so they will have the best chance of passing examinations.

My observations conform to the picture in the literature. The home is left in the care of the wife, and the husband is absent most of the week. There are, however, several gaps in the picture. In the first place, the literature agrees that the company has replaced the extended family and village society for the men—it now provides economic security, a focus for complete lifetime loyalty, recreational outlets, and human relationships in which the salary man can seek advice about personal problems from his work superiors. It often provides housing, stores, and help with children's education—or even finding a marriage partner. On the other hand, the literature seems to point to a gradual separation of the housewife from anything resembling a community.[3] If this is true, the urban housewife should find it difficult to make friends and must face many of the crises of life without social support. Not only will she have to deal with the daily problems of the household and child care by herself; she will also be obliged to handle sickness, death, domestic problems, and financial emergencies without help or advice from others. Further, separated by the walls of her home from common activity with women in similar situations, she will be deprived of opportunities to learn by example how to deal with such problems.

Even cursory glances at city and ward newsletters, newspaper advertisements, and billboards reveal that there are a variety of women's groups—some hobby oriented, some study, some civic service. Moreover, Japanese social commentators as well as government officials make frequent use of the English word "community" in debates over the effect of urban life on the traditional relationships of mutual dependence supposedly exemplified by the extended family and the rural village. As in other societies, the family system seems threatened. Questions of how to build "community" in urban Japan are debated by scholars, social critics, and government officials. These issues added to the questions in my mind. If care of the family and home is primarily the responsibility of the housewife, and if questions are being raised about "community" in urban Japan, why could I find no indication of the relation of the housewife to the community or even any desire for a community? Do the various women's groups serve this function? What are the functions of these groups, and are they primarily neighborhood oriented? Who joins what and why? And who does not?

There is another unanswered issue from the woman's point of view. What importance, if any, does the type of housing have for a woman's formation of social relationships outside the family? Many studies questioning the breakdown of community relate the phenomenon of *danchi* living to the isolation of the housewife and family. (See, for example, Kiefer 1968 and Morioka 1968.) Works on the salary man indicate that company housing can place great stress on the housewife surrounded by people connected to her husband's job. If the home is the workplace of the housewife and she spends most of her time there, might it not then be shaping the way she relates to others around her? Conversations with Japanese women as well as reading on human relationships and housing in other societies strengthened my impression of the importance of housing in this regard. (See, for example, Festinger et al. 1950 and Whyte 1956.)

A number of changes have occurred in Japan to help shape this study. In the 1970s there was an increase in citizens' movements against pollution and proposed developments that would lower their standard of living. (See, for example, McKean 1981.) Furthermore, there has been a marked rise in labor-force participation by married women, the press has paid greater attention to women's group actitivities, and there has been a growing demand for such activity by women.

In this study I examine the behavior of the housewives in my sample as well as their definitions of community and civic involvement. In the process I deal with the following issues: What does the housewife's role set include and how does it change during her life cycle? What social constraints are placed on the housewife? What are the mechanisms she uses to deal with role strain, and what structurally induced motivations and structural alternatives are available to her?[4] What are her reference groups? And, finally, what is the importance of the housing milieu in which she lives? We must consider this variable along with age, education, and income because the home is the housewife's place of work and the place where she spends a great deal of time. Furthermore, as the husband's social life is separate from that of the wife, the home may play an increasingly important role in shaping the way she meets people and determining her status. Indeed, the home may even serve as a source of identity in the sense of a woman being considered a *danchi* wife or a *shataku* (company housing) resident. Japanese women themselves tell me that housing is indeed an important variable.

I hope this study will contribute to the literature on reference groups as well as the sociology of the housewife and Japanese society. Although it is confined to a suburb of Tokyo in 1977–1978, it should add a piece, however small, to the jigsaw puzzle of urban community theory.

2 The Community

The term "community" has a number of common meanings. While it often refers to an area of civic administration, it may include such wide-ranging meanings as a group of persons having some feature in common (such as a community of scholars); a housing project, a small town, or suburb as opposed to a big city; and a group emphasizing either affective relations (the neighborhood community) or instrumental relations (community schools, community waterworks). In all cases it is a sort of identification. Communities have members and should have boundaries, though not necessarily geographical. The community of the individual in traditional society is often described as being clearly defined, with geographical and interpersonal boundaries coinciding. In some cases this traditional "community" is given the attribute of warmth and affectivity.[1] In contrast, the urban dweller's "community" is not so clear-cut. A person may belong to one group in terms of civic administration, to another in terms of workplace, and to yet another in terms of friends, family, and so forth. This image is characterized by instrumental relationships and less warmth but greater individual freedom.

These two images, one warm, the other cold, are used not only by social scientists but also by planners and social workers, and they frequently appear in the media. Governments try to prevent the "breakdown of community," social scientists discover that it exists in rundown neighborhoods (See Gans 1962b and Suttles 1972), and the press discusses the loneliness of the urban dweller.

Unsuccessful development projects have shown that it is not enough to build structures, put people in them, and say this is your new community. Rather the social reality must be taken into consideration. As Albert Hunter (1974, 7) argues:

For meaningful social action to take place individuals need some organizing principle, some "definition of the situation" which includes a spatial referent . . . that for local urban communities to operate as objects and arenas of meaningful social action their residents must possess some conceptual image of them . . . that these symbolic images must be shared or collective representations, and that individuals must have the means, varying needs, and abilities to draw on this local culture to define and delimit meaningful symbolic communities.

To include all possible dimensions, in this study, "community" refers to that sphere within the boundaries of which lie the solidarity-producing institutions and the informal primary relationships of the persons who recognize themselves as its members. By looking at the variety of personal and associational-relationships of the urban housewife and limiting the population to a single suburb of Tokyo, I will show the range and variety of these relationships, the constraints and motivations involved, and the alternatives available as well as the fluctuations over the life cycle. Thus I hope to contribute to an understanding of the concept of urban community in the wider sense, including the three dimensions of solidarity institutions, primary interaction, and institutionally distinct groups cited by Marcia Effrat (1974, 2–3).

During the last decade or so, the English term "community" has appeared increasingly in the Japanese press and in the speech of politicians and city officials. It carries the image of a search for warm relationships in cold urban society. This term is being used not only because it is a fashionable Western word but also to avoid such Japanese terms as *kyōdōtai,* which carry with them traditional images of the type of human network involved.[2]

Although there is debate over the nature of the *kyōdōtai* as it existed in the past (see Irokawa 1975 and Kamishima 1961), the term has connotations of hierarchy, involuntary membership based on residence, continuity of member families over generations, and cooperation in a variety of functional areas.[3] As in the West, increased mobility related to the modernization/industrialization process has weakened some of these traditional structures, and the rootlessness and freedom of urban residents as well as their need for some type of solidarity have become the subject of serious study. (See, for example, Irokawa 1975, Nakamura 1973, Dore 1958, Okuda 1977, and Takabatake 1975.) This contemporary type of solidarity involves a greater consideration of the individuality of the members, more emphasis on horizontal rather than vertical (hierarchical) relationships, and the responsibility of local residents to deal with local problems rather than expecting the government to take care of everything. (See Nakamura 1973.) The two elements distinguishing this new image from that of the *kyōdōtai* are the lack of hierarchy and permanence among members and a voluntary spirit of cooperation.

Some observers argue that this voluntary spirit will develop as people settle into permanent residences and face common threats such as pollution.[4] In response to these threats, citizens' movements may develop and social relationships may evolve. (See, for example, Takabatake 1975, Asukada 1965, and Matsubara 1971.) These observers do not indicate how people who do not own homes or those who are frequently transferred will fit into such solidarity relationships. Moreover, they ignore the possibility that citizens' movements may be no more than a temporary response to a crisis and will break apart when the crisis ends. (See, for example, Takabatake 1973.) Finally, only a small percentage of people are actually involved in citizens' movements.[5]

Nakamura (1973) indicates the difficulties encountered by most people in dealing with the exigencies of work and family alone. Only those who are especially fortunate in terms of resources or energy can find the time to involve themselves in local government. He also questions whether common interests can be assumed from common residential area and whether, even though the neighborhood may be the best unit for administering certain services, it is essential that residents have a high degree of contact with their neighbors. Other groups of people, such as workmates, classmates, and friends, may help to prevent loneliness in the city. It is important, therefore, to look closely at the fit between the functions of the formal civic-structures and those of other formal and informal relationships.

One type of formal organization that was associated with the *kyōdōtai* and still exists today is the *chōnaikai,* or block association.[6] Another is the self-governing association *(jichikai).* The *chōnaikai* is based on the division of a ward, city, or town into blocks; the *jichikai* is usually formed among the residents of a housing project. Both organizations deal with the exigencies of residential life—local festivals, sharing expenses for common water or lighting facilities, calling on members to cooperate in cleaning the local garbage disposal area, or weeding the housing project lawn. In such organizations, membership is by household, not by individual, and is virtually compulsory for residents. There are a wide variety of functions. The groups also function as the lowest level of administration, although they are not government organizations and may even oppose the government and take quite radical positions if the interests of the residents so demand. (See Nakamura 1973, 95–97.) The leadership of such organizations rotates in principle from household to household in order. As Nakamura (1973, 95) indicates, however, *chōnaikai* are often controlled by a clique of long-term residents living in their own homes.[7]

Dore (1958, 257) suggests that the importance of this type of formal organization declines as the resident's work-related activities come to be located outside the residential area. One factor preserving such neighborhood relations is the desire to see friendly, rather than hostile, faces outside the door. Since the demands placed on the member households are usually not very heavy anyway, it is usually preferable to take one's turn rather than alienate neighbors by refusing.

Recent work by Bestor (1985) indicates that the continued survival of *chōnaikai* represents more than remnants of tradition. On the one hand, the *chōnaikai* continues to have a generally conservative attitude and carry out the tasks requested by the local government. On the other hand, it resists local government attempts to redirect community loyalties to a higher (ward or city) level and makes use of neighborhood history and customs to work for the maintenance of a neighborhood community identity. From the point of view of community formation, it is interesting to note that both local governments and residents' associations (whether older *chōnaikai* or newer *jichikai*) make use of traditionalistic activities such as festivals to foster community consciousness.

In examining informal relations, Dore (1958, 262–268) found that some housewives indicated that neighbors were closer than relatives. He also observed neighbors lending and borrowing and giving one another character references. The two limiting factors on such relations were personality and physical presence in the neighborhood for the majority of the day. When men work outside the neighborhood during the day and women work within it, one would expect to find a difference in the importance of both formal and informal neighborhood relations for men and for women.

Okuda (1977) contrasts the bases of formal and informal interpersonal relations. The formal relationship of coresidents (the *jichikai*) is based on their being the recipients of common services. It is a relationship characterized by emphasis on "my home,"[8] with protection of privacy the foremost concern of the residents.[9] Informal relations, he believes, will be more selective, with people maintaining their privacy while selecting friends from a variety of categories, including neighbors. Friendships tend to be based on specific problems or functions, such as the local environment or work. The ability to be selective in informal relations requires preservation of privacy and is exemplified by the construction of public halls and common rooms in housing complexes. (The use of common rooms is discussed in Chapters 5 and 8.) Okuda optimistically hopes these informal relationships will lead to neighbors taking an active part in improving their residential environment.

Survey data indicate that residents participate more in festivals, sports, and other recreational activities than in *jichikai, chōnaikai,* PTA, women's groups, senior citizen's organizations, and the like.[10] What people want from their residential area are opportunities to engage in recreational activities with their neighbors and to talk with one another. They see the neighborhood as a place for a change of scene or for relieving stress. There is a demand for facilities that will enable them to use their neighborhood in this way.

The importance of residence-related community may depend on the status of the resident.[11] A full-time housewife may find that the amount of time she spends and number of roles she plays in the neighborhood make it of greater importance to her than to her husband who works outside. The literature suggests that the worlds of men (work-related) and women (home-related) are far more separate in Japan than in much of the West.[12] This divergence leads to separate networks of communication for the wife and husband: The wife develops a consciousness of residing in a given area or neighborhood, and the husband becomes more involved in a wider network. (See Wazaki 1965, 166–167.) The married woman who moves into a neighborhood where she has no friends may feel isolated until she joins a formal organization such as the PTA, through which she begins to relate to her neighborhood. (See Vogel 1967, 102–141.) Her neighborhood contacts, however, are not just social; they are also functional and relate to her role as wife and mother. It behooves the wife, then, to keep up such contacts and contribute whatever is required to be considered a member of her neighborhood.

To investigate that residence-related community is more important for the full-time housewife than for her husband who works outside, I conducted my study within the boundaries of one suburban city. Identification with that city and with the neighborhood may therefore be considered among foci for solidarity.

3 The Housewife

A housewife has been defined as "a woman responsible for running her home, whether she performs the tasks herself or hires people to do them" (Lopata 1971, 3). This is the general definition I use here, but I add the further stipulation that only women who have been married at least once are included in the category housewife. The role set of the housewife, regardless of her other activities, encompasses being a wife to her husband, taking charge of the housekeeping tasks, and bearing the main responsibility for child care. Even though men are now taking on some of these tasks few go beyond simple willingness to help their wives. The responsibility is ultimately hers, even in the "dual career family." Regardless of their involvement outside the home, housewives tend to rank roles associated with the home and family higher than other roles and do not have much respect for women who do not. (See Lopata 1971, 47–48, 54.)

Some roles are considered more important, more creative, and less repetitive than others. Cleaning and washing, for example, may be cited as dull and frustrating because they have to be done over and over again, whereas child care is often considered to be creative. Women often cite child care as the reason why they must stay home, and frequently it is the source of the housewife's greatest satisfaction (as well as her greatest frustrations). It can be seen as tying the woman to the home and keeping her from work or other activities. Even though there is a great demand for child-care facilities, the heavy responsibility of training a future adult and developing a child's character makes it difficult to leave these tasks in the hands of others.

Helena Lopata's study leaves the impression of a housewife who views the world from the perspective of her family. Even in evaluating her spouse, whom she may have married for a variety of reasons other than being a good breadwinner or potential father, she tends to place family-related roles first.

Certainly the vast majority of Japanese women marry. By the age of fifty, 98 percent of Japanese women have been married, and 37 percent of Japanese women over the age of fifteen are housewives.[1] Studies done in the 1950s depict the Japanese housewife as being more single-handedly responsible for the household than her American counterpart. (See Dore 1958 and Vogel 1967.) In particular, the urban, salaryman husband is depicted as leaving home early and coming back late. He expects the housework to be done and does not wish to be bothered by tasks around the home. The wife's duty is to see that he can rest for the next day's work.

Very little overlap occurs between the two worlds of home and work. The husband has his friends and colleagues, and they tend to gather in bars or restaurants after work or on the golf course on weekends. The wife's friends are mainly in the neighborhood, and often they do not know one another's husbands.

Marriage in Japan is extremely stable. The divorce rate, while rising, is low,[2] and despite the acceptance of the "love marriage,"[3] personal affection between husband and wife is less important than making a home and family. George DeVos (1973, 10–11) writes:

> Role behavior within the family has remained relatively cohesive and relatively satisfying for individual Japanese. The emphasis on the formal role one is expected to play in the immediate family and in external relationships has seemed, to some Western observers at least, in general more extreme than that found in Western societies. What is, in our opinion, extreme is not the playing of roles (which one finds everywhere) but the degree to which the sense of a personal self has been deemphasized in Japanese culture.

This same phenomenon is described by Takie Sugiyama Lebra (1976b, chaps. 2 and 5) as the importance for the Japanese of "belongingness" and "occupying the proper place." She further argues that Japanese are very status-oriented, which carries over into conspicuous display of status in terms of goods, club memberships, and so forth. There is also much concern with what she calls "status propriety"—behaving like the holder of one's status (*onna rashii,* "like a woman"). This propriety includes external appearance: The occupant of a status not only is supposed to act in a certain way but is supposed to *look* like the occupant of that status. (See Lebra 1976b, 69–79.)

How is the housewife supposed to look? The traditional model of a woman who subordinates all other activity to the wife and mother role and leaves working outside to her husband seems to be changing. In this case the division of labor is clear-cut and the roles of husband and wife are not interchangeable. Although such housewives still exist, a second type of housewife, the "new woman," has developed. While accepting the traditional assumption of the centrality of the domestic role, the new woman believes that she should also be able to engage in activities unrelated to the homemaker role. Women may now work outside and men may help around the house; but for the women, home takes priority whereas for the men, work does. One factor accounting for the appearance of this new woman is the change that has taken place in the Japanese woman's life course since World War II. (See Figure 1.) Not only has her life expectancy increased by almost 26 years, but the period of childbearing has contracted from 12 years to 2.6 years. She is receiving more years of education and is marrying later. Even ignoring changes in housekeeping practices and laborsaving devices, today's woman spends less time carrying out the obligations of childbearing and child care than her predecessors. A third type is the woman who denies that the home is the woman's responsibility by virtue of her sex alone. Such women are still few in number.[4]

The perception of sex roles seems also to be changing. In 1972 there was 80 percent support for the proposition that the husband should work outside and the wife should take care of the home. This high degree of support came from both men and women.[5] In 1976, however, only 48.8 percent of the women surveyed agreed with this proposition.[6] Disagreement was strongest among women with higher education and also among younger women. When the same question was asked of a nationwide sample of leaders and intellectuals (including university professors, lawyers, and leaders of women's groups), there was only 20 percent support for the proposition and 64 percent opposition (83 percent of the women versus 45 percent of the men). (See "Otoko wa shigoto" 1978.) Activity outside the home has apparently become a socially acceptable option for women. Whether or not they expect their daughters to hold a paying job, more and more mothers are interested in seeing that their daughters have the means to support themselves if necessary. (See, for example, "Chōsa ripōto" 1977, 91.)

Apart from work, a variety of alternative activities are available. Housewives have become involved in political activity, consumer

Figure 1. Life Cycle of the Average Japanese Woman

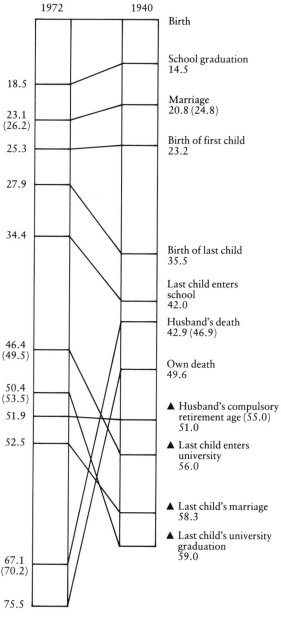

Source: Foreign Press Center of Japan (1977).
Note: Numbers denote age and the symbol ▲ signifies
events after death in the 1940 case; husband's age is
given in parentheses.

movements, and government-sponsored adult education courses.[7] These activites are seen not merely as a way of passing time but as essential if women are to understand the problems of society. (See, for example, "Himatsubushi de wa arimasen" 1978.)

Do these and other alternatives lead to status conflict for the Japanese housewife? Despite the increasing number of alternatives, the question remains, as this book will show, one of status competition, not status conflict.[8] Furthermore, what has been described as extreme role commitment or lack of a personal self may reflect the recurrent periods of family involvement that occur over the life course of the Japanese housewife. (See Chapter 5.)

The image of the married woman giving priority to home and family is emphasized in mass media accounts of the successful housewife who also has a professional career. These accounts always take pains to present the way the woman manages to carry out all her domestic duties while she works. A *Nihon Keizai Shinbun* series on working housewives included the following examples.[9] A housewife who became a tax specialist began her study after her last child was in kindergarten, studied via correspondence courses, and took five years to pass all the examinations. She rearranged and cleaned the entire house before she began her first job so that her family would not be inconvenienced by her working; she asked the other women in her neighborhood for help; and she continues to cook and run the house while holding down a full-time job. A second housewife looked around for something to occupy her time when her third child turned three. She decided to study law. Since she could not leave the family long enough to study at a university, she enrolled in a correspondence course and studied during the gaps in her housework. After passing the law examinations she told her husband, who replied "Oh, really?" Only after he agreed, however, did she determine to go on with the necessary study and also take a job. She managed the home with the help of a housekeeper but retained the ultimate responsibility; she is only able to continue her work and study because her family has not suffered. This newspaper series dealt with outstanding women who seem to have boundless energy. Although I do not focus on such women, the emphasis on managing both home and work does require a further look at the degree of acceptance of the principle that the housewife must manage her home and family before she may engage in an outside activity.

The importance of family roles is given further support by data on the housewife's feelings of satisfaction. Iwao Sumiko (1976, 63ff.) finds that women, asked how they could improve their lives, said they would choose first of all to teach their hobbies and crafts to a group (25.7 percent). This finding reflects their desire to engage in an activity that does not require much time or does not interfere with the family but does provide some income. When younger women with children were asked how they would improve their lives, they responded that they wanted to be better wives and mothers (15.5 percent for the entire sample). "To find a good job" was the response of 14.2 percent of the sample as a whole, which fits in with the increasing participation of married women in the labor force described in following chapters. Far behind was the desire to improve one's life by participation in civic or consumer movements (1.3 percent). Lastly, 20 percent of the women did not want to do anything in particular to improve their lives. This attitude differed with age, ranging from 9 percent for those between eighteen and twenty-four years of age to 47 percent for those over sixty.

Iwao also points out that over a twenty-year period (1953–1973) Japanese women's attitudes toward the position of women have become more positive. In 1953, some 64 percent of women interviewed preferred to be born as men versus 27 percent who preferred to be born as women. In 1973 this proportion changed to 43 percent preferring to be men as opposed to 50 percent preferring to be women. In 1953, moreover, 39 percent of women respondents felt that men faced more difficulties than women whereas 42 percent thought the opposite. In 1973, there was a more favorable view of women's position: 47 percent of women respondents said men's life was more difficult versus 34 percent who said women's life. (See Iwao n.d., 95–111.)

Michael Berger (1976) argues that four factors enter into the Japanese woman's positive evaluation of her role. First, Japanese society defines both the roles assigned to men and those to women as important. Second, Japanese women are rather skeptical about the man's world, especially the white-collar world. Third, "few Japanese women seem to have any feelings of inferiority in their all-important emotional relations with men" (p. 57). Fourth, increasing numbers of women are finding that a broader life-style is possible and "housewife" is not a dirty word.

The argument that there is a positive image of the housewife is reinforced by Hara Hiroko, who points to the ways in which the housewife can attain prestige in her local neighborhood, her relative autonomy in dealing with the family budget, and her responsibility in dealing with the personal relationships of importance to her family. (See Berger 1976, 58.) In arts and culture, activities may be regarded as mere pastimes, a means of gaining prestige, or a sign that one has the time and money to permit such luxuries. On the other hand, one might question, as some women do, whether such activities are any less valuable than the daily work of a husband who sits and "stamps papers all day." (See Berger 1976, 63.)

Women may also question whether their husbands are really satisfied with the tasks they perform all day. Is the male work world indeed an ideal to be emulated, or is men's work "important" simply because men say it is? Is it not possible that women's work is equally satisfying and that civic, social, and cultural activities might be at least as important outlets for energy as the work men do in offices and factories? (See Berger 1976.)

Finally, there is the question of the lasting contributions of the roles of men and women. Men, away from home and family for a great deal of the time, may in fact spend most of their lives doing fairly routine tasks to be replaced at retirement by other men who will spend the same sort of lives. Women, on the other hand, may have a greater personal influence in their families. This evaluation is expressed by one Japanese housewife as follows (Berger 1976, 67): "I don't know which is better, working or being closer to home, but in my family, our grandmother played a central role, influenced our values, our education, and therefore our lives, and was deeply respected by all of us. I wonder if she did not leave a more profound legacy than our grandfather, who woked hard all his life but never really got to know us."

However this may be on the individual level, from the societal perspective there is, as Yoshida and Kanda (1977) point out, a strongly held consensus that women should give first priority to the home irrespective of the question of whether individual women find their purposes in life within the family or not. In other words, society is not ambivalent about the roles of women, although individual women themselves may feel ambivalent.

The role of the Japanese housewife has been called a "profession"—a full-time, lifelong career to which she is expected to commit herself just as her husband is expected to commit himself to his work. The interdependence of the husband's and wife's roles in this division of labor is said to be merely a manifestation of the interdependence that characterizes Japanese society as a whole, not something unique to the sex-role division of labor. (See Vogel 1978, 16–17.)

The main task of the housewife is mothering both her children and her husband, who turns to her for emotional support but is unable in turn to help her with her responsibilities. (See Vogel 1978 and Ōhara 1976, 24–27.) If the wife is tired and unable to give the husband the soothing he desires, he will be annoyed and suggest that she cut down on outside activities. Conserving her energies for the primary tasks of running the home, mothering, and comforting is the wife's major duty. Other activities may be permitted so long as they do not make her less effective as a nurturer, and certainly other activities are to be avoided if they mean that she might require any nurturing herself.[10]

In Japanese society, the mother's physical presence is thought to be extremely important; indeed, the cry of a child is regarded as proof that mother should not leave him alone.[11] On the other hand, so long as mother is present, it is quite permissible for father to be gone for months or even years for business reasons.

Children's education is based on the premise that mother will be free to devote a lot of time to helping the child—not only with homework and at examination time but making nutritious and varied lunches, seeing that the child does not forget to bring items to school, ensuring that he has a clean handkerchief and clean fingernails every day, and so on. Teachers often send home a memo asking the mother to produce a box or case or other item made to a specified size by the next day. A Japanese woman professor told me of all the spur-of-the-moment demands from her son's school. She was expected, for example, to make cases for several of his pieces of equipment including his harmonica. Since she had neither the time nor a great deal of skill in sewing, she always had to pay someone to produce these items on demand. And if the items fail to meet specifications, they may be returned to the mother, as happened when the cord for the child's harmonica case was too long.

A further example of school expectation appeared in a shopping column of *The Japan Times*. A fruit wholesaler preferred to bring home fruit at the peak of its flavor, rather than the first offerings of any particular fruit. He was informed by his son's kindergarten teacher that only his son among all the children had not yet brought cherries in his lunchbox. Several discussions with Japanese women indicate that schoolteachers say that children of working mothers have dirty fingernails.

Mothers are expected to participate in PTA, which meets during the day (making it difficult for the working woman), and take their turns at various offices in this group. There is also a great deal of after-school learning that involves mothers, whether it is taking children to art, music, or sports lessons or to after-school academic study to help them pass the extremely difficult examinations as they move from compulsory (through high junior school) to noncompulsory (high school and above) education. The mother's assistance at examination time is seen as essential emotional support even when it is limited to fixing snacks and tea for the student. There are a number of cook-books on the market specializing in nutritious food for students study-ing for examinations. (These books are aimed at the mother, of course, who is supposed to have time to make the elaborate items pic-tured within.) One September, a housewife informed me that she could no longer join the graduates of her cooking class in their occa-sional gathering because her daughter was studying for examinations —in the spring.

It is thus not surprising, as Vogel points out, that the mother views the child's success at school as *her* achievement. Other mothers will come to consult with the mother of a child who has done well on a dif-ficult examination and entered a prestigious school. This desire to see their children (as their products) succeed in school may motivate mothers to join adult education classes or even *mama-juku* (training schools) to help them help their children.

Thus, the presence of children at home is a strong reason to keep the housewife physically close at hand and available to anticipate their every need. And when the children leave home, it is time for the hus-band to retire. His needs and his unwillingness to be left alone have the same effect as the child's—making the wife feel that her presence is absolutely essential for the family and a crucial aspect of her career. (See Vogel 1978, 35.)

Another aspect of the housewife's role set relates to her representa-tion of husband and family to the outside world. Usually it is the wife who maintains the ties with relatives, neighbors, or benefactors, selects gifts or writes cards at appropriate times, and is expected to build up her husband's image, especially by giving him credit for any accomplishments of the family. (See Vogel 1978, 28–29.) This acquiescence reflects the housewife's position as her husband's representative, having final authority neither with respect to the children nor with respect to society at large. It also means that she is able to take responsibility when it suits her and evade it when it does not. (See Ōhara 1976, 24–27.) She has an escape route in being able to say she must ask her husband's permission or that she does not know about something. This excuse is not generally used unless she wants to escape from an onerous decision or task. Rather than being interpreted as weakness, it may well be a mechanism preserved by housewives themselves to avoid the burdens that come with responsibility.

In the light of Suzanne Vogel's finding (1978, 33) that the wife feels hampered if the husband is around too much, it becomes difficult to use the excuse that one must consult one's husband if the husband is in fact present. It also is difficult to act with authority as representative of one's husband (while in fact making the relevant decisions on one's own initiative) if the husband is indeed present. Thus too much involvement of the husband may undermine both the wife's authority and her ability to maintain an escape route from onerous duties. By evading final responsibility, of course, the housewife may also have to resort to achieving vicariously through husband or children or give them credit even though she may have done all the work. The attribution of final responsibility to one's husband may be one of the ways in which housewives try to alleviate role strain. Rather than delegating responsibility, she does not acknowledge it, even though in fact she is responsible for the task. This means a reduction in the strain at the cost of the rights and privileges that accompany the position of authority.

Other means of coping with role strain include defining behavior as gender-appropriate and compartmentalization. For example, it may be acceptable to be a leader in a woman's group because the group's activities are essentially defined as gender-appropriate (compatible with the roles of wife and mother). As for compartmentalization, women may screen their activities from their friends and families. Their reluctance to inform their husbands may include even "legitimately" feminine activities so that the husband will not blame the wife's fatigue on too much outside activity and ask that she devote more time to the home. Activities may also be timed so that they correspond to suitable periods in the woman's life. Voluntary activities may be preferred because, unlike employment, they are flexible and may be combined with the demands of the wife-mother role and abandoned when there are conflicts. (See Pharr 1981, chap. 6.) Meetings may be missed if a child is sick; the mother may quit the organization if the family objects. The voluntary nature of such activities gives a clear definition of priorities: Family comes first.

Even though the housewife can find ways to engage in activities outside the home without questioning the priority of her family roles, many women are reluctant to become involved outside the home. Women give three major reasons for their lack of interest in such activities: no time, no opportunity, and unwillingness to place any burden on the family by going out and thus causing the situation in the home to deteriorate. (See "Chōsa ripōto" 1977.) The study from which these points were taken suggests that it is the lack of contact with others outside their homes that makes women reluctant to involve themselves in various activities. This suggestion is supported by data from a 1974 study by the Prime Minister's Office indicating that women's small social networks cut down on communication. Lack of awareness of activities or of other women like themselves may explain why some women fail to participate in citizens' movements and the like. (See Fujin ni Kansuru 1974, 321–322.)

According to Higuchi Keiko (1975), the PTA experience may draw women out of the home and into other activities. Women are given a chance to use their own identities and are not just so-and-so's mother or wife. Moreover, the PTA gives women a chance to meet people from a variety of backgrounds. This contact with others not only serves as a channel for information but provides a chance to work together on newsletter production, accounting, publicity, and the like. All of this experience teaches the woman new skills and shows her where different sources of information are located in her area.

As Higuchi points out, this experience may give a woman more leadership training than her husband receives, or at least she may receive it at an earlier age. Since women "retire" from the PTA when their last child graduates from junior high school, they may then be encouraged to use the skills they have learned in other organizations. While still active in the PTA they may form other groups for social or political activity. The PTA teaches such women how to organize and how best to approach their problems. At the very least it offers women a chance to meet others and open channels of communication.

Another study shedding light on women involved in outside activity is Kiyohara Keiko's work on the leaders of the home library movement (1978).[12] She found that some 60 percent of the leaders are between the ages of thirty-five and thirty-nine; all are housewives; the majority have two children but 36 percent have three children; 60 percent have children between the ages of three and nine, and 60 percent have a child below the age of six. In terms of education, all of the leaders had progressed beyond junior high school. Some 43.4 percent were high school graduates, 13.2 percent were graduates of technical schools *(senmongakko)*, 9.4 percent were graduates of junior colleges, and 32.1 percent were graduates of four-year colleges. Although 81.1 percent had work experience, only 13.2 percent were working at the time of the study. Since husbands were almost all employed and away from home during the daytime, the wives did not have to clarify how they used their spare time.

Women joined most often for the sake of their own children, but even when their children grew up, the group's leaders stayed on for the sake of the neighborhood children. In other words, there was a transformation of consciousness: They began by joining the group because it was an opportunity for their children but ended up participating in it as a regional organization. Participation led these women to petition the city to improve library services and obtain funding for their movement. This is an example of how joining an activity for the sake of her own family can involve the housewife in broader activities. Some 66 percent of these leaders had taken part in adult education classes, mostly motivated by the desire to improve their skills within the movement—for example, they studied children's literature and story telling. All this participation meant increased time outside the home. Lastly, some 75 percent of these leaders had participated in some other social activity, including PTA and food co-ops.

There is, then, evidence of change from the traditional image of the housewife. At the same time, there is evidence of strong family-centeredness. The investigation of the housewife's community must begin with a clarification of the functions of family and those of the outside world. It must also include a clearer indication of the role models available to the contemporary housewife and any restraints placed on her involvement outside the home.

4   Santama City and Its Inhabitants

My investigation took place in 1977–1978 in a suburb of Tokyo which I will call Santama City. I chose the location because it included a number of city-run centers that offered not only a variety of activities but also facilities for citizens who organized their own activities. Numerous women's and residents' groups were active in the area, and all categories of housing I intended to investigate were present and in close proximity.[1]

Through Professor Aoi Kazuo of the University of Tokyo I obtained introductions that led to access to city-run centers, the community center, and a variety of materials and data. Santama City was interested in building civic spirit among its residents and was in the process of building community centers to foster this spirit. This drive gave an added dimension to my study. The idea of civic spirit was well publicized, residents were being asked their opinions about these new centers, and an effort was under way to portray Santama City as the residents' "community." Since my inquiries would not appear outlandish to either residents or city officials, I could hope for cooperation, and the community center and other resident facilities would provide a location for research and meeting housewives.

To gather both qualitative and quantitative data, I designed a three-stage project: participant observation in the community center for a period of four months; in-depth interviews with housewives and community leaders; and a survey administered to a stratified random sample of housewives over the age of twenty-five. Details of my methodology are given in the appendix.

Characteristics of Santama City

Santama City is located on the western side of the Tokyo metropolitan area. It underwent rapid growth as an industrial and residential suburb after World War II. The city covers an area of 16.83 square kilometers and has a population of slightly over 160,000.[2] Originally a farming settlement, it received an influx of residents engaged in other occupations during the postwar period. Between 1950 and 1960, the population increased from 54,198 to 92,090, and by 1970 it had risen to 149,113. The city's convenient location on the Chūō Line (one of the major commuting lines connected to central Tokyo) and its network of buses to three major commuting stations, as well as access to a major park, made the area an attractive site for "bedtown" development. This explosive population increase has settled since 1970, however, and the yearly increase recorded January 1, 1974, was only 1.01 percent. This settling of the population has allowed the city to turn its attention toward building a civic spirit. Although the numbers vary slightly from district to district, the majority of residents have moved to Santama City since 1960, making a population of relatively recent residents. The population is young in years as well as period of residence. At the time of this study, 68 percent of the population were under the age of forty and 28 percent were under twenty. In the case of women, 66.3 percent were under forty and 28 percent were under twenty. Comparable national figures were 31 percent under twenty and 63 percent under forty and, for women, 29 percent under twenty and 61.9 percent under forty.

At the time of the study, 1.5 percent of the working population were in primary industries, 39.1 percent in secondary, and 59.4 percent in tertiary; 60 percent of the 74,559 employed persons worked outside the city. The average length of commuting time was forty-six minutes one way. When occupation is analyzed by sex, approximately 61 percent of the women over twenty appear to be housewives versus 22 percent who are employed. (The rest were either students, unemployed, or other.) Annual income figures for the period indicate that 6 percent of Santama City residents had an income under 1 million yen, 24 percent between 1 and 2 million yen, 31 percent between 2 and 3 million yen, 17 percent between 3 and 4 million yen, and 19 percent over 4 million yen. These figures compare with the national average annual income at the time of 2.2 million yen for an employed individual.

In terms of housing, 40 percent of the residents owned and 60 percent rented their present dwellings. This finding contrasts with the national average of 59 percent owned and 40 percent rented. Housing type is reflected in community identification; a higher percentage of homeowners (46.5 percent) than renters (33.7 percent) identified themselves as Santama citizens. A higher percentage of renters (44.3 percent) than homeowners (30.6 percent) identified themselves as Tokyo citizens.

There is a strong desire to stay in Santama City if possible: 75 percent of those polled wanted to stay in contrast to 10 percent who wanted to move. The desire to move or stay differed with the type of housing. Persons in their own home or in public housing wanted to stay, whereas those in rented houses or private apartments wanted to leave. The most frequently given reasons for wanting to stay were good environment (37 percent), fondness for the area because of long residence (36 percent), and convenient transportation (13 percent). Reasons given for wanting to move were housing situation (37 percent), bad environment (29 percent), and transportation or work-related factors (25 percent).

It is in this environment that the city is making efforts to develop a civic spirit. Long-time residents have a stronger identification than newcomers as Santama citizens. At the same time, most people think that the government should do whatever needs to be done. When asked about their neighborhood contacts (three houses opposite and one on either side), residents replied: "Greet one another when we meet" (33.1 percent), "stand and talk to one another outside our homes" (30.5 percent), "go shopping and so forth together" (18.4 percent), "ask favors and borrow items or money" (13.0 percent), and "no relation whatsoever" (4.3 percent). Relationships beyond "standing and talking" are in the minority.

Government surveys show that residents do not wish to increase contact with their neighbors; rather, they prefer to leave the task of improving their living environment to neighborhood self-governing organizations. This attitude is said to reflect the fact that most husbands commute to work in Tokyo and are members of the self-governing associations in name only. The actual work in civic affairs is left to the housewives.

The city government decided to build several community centers as a means of fostering civic spirit. Their rationale in doing so was to overcome the residents' apathy and their tendency to expect the city government to solve their problems for them. The concept of "community" was, the city administration contended, unfamiliar to the ordinary resident, a term that people merely half-understood. In this light, the administration sought to emphasize that "community," or a spirit of identity among residents of an area, must grow from the grass roots and cannot be handed down by the government. To develop such a spirit, residents must do more than merely seek to avoid the old local *kyōdōtai;* they must begin, rather, to plan new sorts of associations. This is necessary because individual families cannot solve such problems as pollution, juvenile delinquency, or care of the aged. These problems must be solved on a local level, the city argues, and residents must take responsibility for the duties that accompany their rights as citizens. Women, the city continues, are the source of civic activity, and it is through such activity that they perceive the connection between themselves and their families and society at large. To create a good environment for their family, women must take a greater role in their community.

To bring about all this change and to increase residents' interest in their neighborhood *(chiiki),* the city government plans to build seven community centers. These centers will include a local park, an athletic field, a gymnasium, a coffee shop and light meal service, welfare facilities, facilities for children, a library, and an adult education center. Citizens are expected to participate in the development of community centers. The city provides funds and land and explains the limitations on building, but the residents are to decide for themselves what sort of facilities, layout, and the like they want with the funds available. For this planning to be carried out, the city provides a place to meet and calls a general meeting of local residents, who then elect representatives to work out the details. After the center is built, management of the facility is placed in the hands of the residents.

By June 1979 three community centers had been built. One had been open only two months; another had been open only fourteen months. Neither center was open when the fieldwork for this study was done. During the first year of operation, the second center made concerted efforts to present a wide variety of activities, study groups, and the like to introduce as many people as possible to the facilities.

Not all of the facilities were completed at the time of opening, however, and the swimming pool was due to open in the summer of 1979. The third community center was the site of the participant observation stage of this research project. It opened in February 1974. An imposing, fortresslike structure of gray concrete, it comprises three stories and an array of facilities. On the ground floor are a restaurant, the office and reception areas, a tatami room (for classes or meetings), a heated pool (closed in the winter because of the prohibitive cost of heating), two rooms for children (one with tables and chairs for reading, crafts, and so on, and one with no furniture but space for free play), a walled-in play area for children in part of the yard (with direct access from the playroom), and all the facilities for management, heating, pool, showers, and so forth. On the second floor are a gymnasium—a lobbylike area that can be used for relaxing or for activities such as dancing—and a library. The top floor houses a projection room, a stereo room, a large meeting room, two large tatami rooms (used primarily by senior citizens and including simple kitchen facilities), and two *furo* (Japanese-style baths) for the free use of senior citizens. On each floor there is hot water for tea or washing dishes. The pool, gymnasium, and library are the most popular facilities. With exception of the pool, more women use the facilities than men. Since large numbers of students and working men commute to locations outside Santama City, they are unable to use the facilities as often as women or little children.

The district itself is one of the more sparsely settled parts of Santama city. In 1979, the district's population was 11,888. It contains a large area used as an astronomical observatory and closed to the public. According to a 1971 survey, 80 percent of the district's residents want to make their permanent home there, so most of the residents have a strong interest in the neighborhood. It is characterized as an area into which future residents of Santama City will move; as yet it is underdeveloped. Hospitals, schools, and so forth are few in number, but such facilities are expected to increase with the population.

In accordance with the basic principle of administration by the residents, the community center is run by a board of directors. Of the ten directors, five are elected from the residents of the district at large and five from the Jūmin Kyōgi Kai, an association of forty-three local residents' groups such as *chōnaikai, jichikai,* and PTA. A city employee acts as office manager because of the necessity of dealing with city funds,[3] and six other employees have been hired from the Jūmin Kyōgi Kai. Under this structure come all the leaders of the various groups using the center. It is not a simple matter to turn such a center over to the management of the local residents, and a number of problems have arisen. Some of the facilities—such as the heated pool in winter and a pub which was originally planned—have just not been feasible to operate. It has also been difficult to meet all the various demands of the local residents. The original hours were to be between 10:30 AM and 9 PM, for instance, but residents wanted the opening time changed to 10 AM. In special cases, the closing time has been extended to 10 PM—for example, to ensure that groups practicing traditional songs and dances do not disturb families living near the local shrine where they previously practiced. Special arrangements were also made for teenagers to practice rock music on days when the center is closed to the general public so they will not disturb the regular users. Although there are many difficulties in administering such a center, flexibility is possible when the residents and not the government are in charge.

Some fifty groups and "circles" with a total of about a thousand members have been formed since the center opened.[4] Although the center has a fairly short history and at the time of the fieldwork there was no other center in Santama City for comparison, it was an excellent site for fieldwork. Observation there helped clarify both the activities in which residents engage and the characteristics of those residents.

The Housewives Studied

Data were collected through in-depth interviews with fifty housewives chosen from the five housing categories mentioned above and with eight civic or activity leaders (including one man), as well as through a questionnaire distributed to a citywide stratified random sample of housewives ($N = 228$). A detailed account of the data collection appears in the appendix.

There are some major differences between the two samples. Some 86 percent of the interviewees were forty-five years of age or under with a concentration (70 percent) between the ages of thirty-one and forty-five. Survey respondents were more widely dispersed. Some 21 percent were between twenty-five and thirty-one years old, 48 percent between thirty-one and forty-five, and 31 percent between forty-six and sixty-one. The greater youth of the interviewees is reflected in their higher level of education (52 percent junior college or more as compared to 38.5 percent for those surveyed) and that of their husbands (74 percent beyond high school in contrast to 55.4 percent of the survey sample). Husbands' occupations reflect these differences in education. Some 70 percent of interviewees' husbands were in professional or white-collar positions in comparison to 55.9 percent of the survey sample husbands. At the time of the study, over 60 percent of both samples was not in the labor force. Family incomes, therefore, were primarily husbands' earnings. These incomes compared quite favorably with Santama City residents' incomes.[5]

The survey respondents were almost equally divided between those who married by *omiai* (arrangement) (43.8 percent) and those who married for love (46.5 percent). The gap was wider for interviewees (22 percent arrangement and 32 percent love). The widest gap was between those who indicated they could not say which type their marriage was (9.7 percent survey, 32 percent interview). This finding reflects the fact that survey respondents were required to choose among the three categories (love, arrangement, or cannot say) whereas interviewees were able to elaborate. Only the older women interviewed and those with little work experience said emphatically that their marriages had been arranged. Women who had met their husbands through work or through friends or relatives after they left school and were working in urban areas usually said theirs were friendly marriages, or "we just fell into marriage" *("nan to naku kekkon shimashita").*

The majority live in nuclear families. Some of the interviewees had lived with parents or in-laws in the past, and some expected to do so in the future. At the time of the study, however, only 24 percent of those surveyed and 12 percent of those interviewed had other relatives living in the household. The vast majority were in their first marriage. Some 3 percent of those surveyed and 4 percent of those interviewed were divorced and remarried—including one interviewee who forcefully said that not even her niece who is married and living in the same apartment building knew she was divorced, suggesting that some divorces or absent husbands may not be reported in the data.

More than two-thirds of both samples do not *believe* in any religion, but there are differences between the samples in terms of type of belief. The survey respondents were more likely (7.9 percent) than interviewees (2 percent) to declare themselves believers in Buddhism. They were slightly less likely to believe in Christianity (6.6 percent survey versus 10 percent interview) and one-third as likely to believe in one of the New Religions (7.9 percent survey versus 22 percent interview).[6] Other characteristics of the samples appear in the chapters that follow.

5 The Life Course

The category "housewife" comprises a variety of women in different family situations. It includes the newly married and childless woman as well as the older woman whose children have left home, although their roles might be very different. The newlywed might be training for future roles as home manager and mother, whereas the older wife might be disengaging from great involvement in the daily lives of her children.

Stages

One approach to this variety is the American life-course typology of Helena Lopata.[1] She delineates four life-course stages. First is the stage of becoming a housewife: Immediately after marriage the young bride, usually untrained for her new role, learns how to be a housewife and reorders her relationships to give priority to life with her husband. Second is the expanding circle: Children are born and, in contrast to the expansion of the family, the wife's sphere of involvement outside the home may be suddenly contracted. The third stage is the full-house plateau: The family is completed but the children have not yet left home, a stage characterized by increasing diversity of life-styles and experimentation with roles. The last stage is the shrinking circle: The children leave home and the housewife's roles shrink.

Lopata points out that American society treats women in the last stage as rather valueless and observes that this phase becomes a gradual retirement compounded by the death of the husband. The woman must disengage from most of the roles she has spent a lifetime perfecting and often has no new active role awaiting her.

Yoshida and Kanda (1977, 35–39) describe a four-stage life course for the contemporary Japanese woman as well: the woman's growth and education; raising the next generation; freedom from the responsibility of raising the next generation; and old age. As in Lopata's America example, their first stage serves as the training period for the second stage but not for anything further. Increased life spans mean that most women are now able to experience the third stage and may spend many years in this phase. Japanese housewives, then, like their American counterparts, may be developing a variety of life-styles and experimenting with new roles during this stage. This experimentation might be reflected in the way the fourth stage is spent or at least preferred to be spent.

Women in these middle years (which begin when the last child enters school) possess "more leisure and greater opportunities for activity outside the home." (See Perry 1976, 221–222.) During this period women receive the greatest prestige for their competence and are at their peak managing the home, even when the mother-in-law is present. This is also a period of demands from children related to their education, future occupation, and marriage.

While certain characteristics of the Japanese housewife's life course may be similar to those of her American counterpart, others may not. Thus we must take a closer look at the housewives under study. Using Lopata's typology, we begin with the first stage: becoming a housewife.

This is the period when women's magazines and television programs relating to household tasks are most avidly followed. Secondary roles may include working until the first child is born and being a companion to one's husband. The husband may bring his friends home and include his wife in his social life. The wife tends to have her most important friendships with former work and school friends, however, and not much connection with her neighborhood. Despite these relationships, the housewife may be extremely busy with her tasks.

Mrs. A, for example, had been married less than a year when interviewed. Her husband is a carpenter, and the family income is 3 million yen a year. She spends most of her time in her apartment. She reads little but prefers newspaper articles on homemaking when she does read. Although she has an interest in becoming a knitting teacher someday, she defines her present role as waiting until a child is born. (She seems to have difficulty in becoming pregnant, or at least she thinks so.)

With a small apartment of just two rooms and a kitchen, she does not have much to do; after her husband leaves in the morning, she goes back to bed until noon. Then she gets up to watch television and clean the house and make dinner before he returns home. Although an aunt who lives in the same apartment building has helped her meet neighborhood women, her friends are from her former job. With her husband's agreement she invites these friends home and sometimes goes out with them in the evening.

Mrs. B had been married only two months when I met her at the home of the woman who acted as honorary go-between in her marriage.[2] She was a graduate of a good four-year university, where she met her husband. He is currently doing graduate work at that university and expects to stay on as a faculty member. She had hoped to continue her job after marriage but gave it up after two months because of household demands. She turned to the marriage go-between (the wife of her husband's professor) for training in the ways of a wife, particularly a faculty wife. She planned to study cooking and sewing during the year or so before she expected their first child to be born. Her decision to give up working was based on the demanding nature of her new husband. She said he was very old-fashioned but also very masculine *(otoko rashii):* "When he gets up in the morning he steps out of his pajamas and just leaves them lying there piled up like chimneys." She continued: "He takes his bath first, of course, and before I can take mine he always asks for something, ice cream or beer maybe."

We turn now to the second stage: the expanding circle. During this period—which refers to the expansion of the family, not the housewife's activities—the woman is most occupied with the physical care of a new infant. She may spend a great deal of time consulting with her mother, mother-in-law, or older siblings to see how they solved childcare problems and how their children measured up to "baby book" standards. Friendships are still primarily with old friends, although they seldom meet. The housewife is disenganging from an active life and shifting toward the neighborhood and, even more important, the child as the center of her existence.

In most cases, the women in this stage had no friends. Most said they were so wrapped up in the baby for the first few months that they did not notice the need for external stimulation. Several said it was not until the second child came along that the uniqueness wore off and they felt the need to get out. There is a gradual disengagement from social activity with the husband. Even the so-called new families—those who supposedly spend leisure time together, frequent family restaurants, shop together, and go for drives—are limited to daytime activities and places where they can take the baby. Rarely does the couple go to a movie or play during this stage. Indeed, there is even doubt whether the "new family" really exists or is just an image created by mass media and advertising.

Most women I interviewed agreed that even if the service were available at prices they could afford, they would not be willing to use a babysitter at night. (Babysitters cost at least 400 yen an hour and usually much more, an amount equal to or greater than the average hourly wage for women working part time; "baby hotels" where children can be looked after by the hour or sometimes by the day or week can run several times this rate.) They were worried that the child would feel lonely, and they felt the mother's physical presence was important.

Mrs. C is married to a man involved in a number of independent businesses, including real estate and restaurant franchises. They have an annual income of about 8 million yen. The mother of a five-month-old boy, she described her day as waking at seven, doing the laundry, getting breakfast, cleaning, getting lunch, preparing the baby's bath, getting dinner, bringing in the laundry, and "in between all that, milk, milk, milk." She had no friends in her condominium, where she had lived for a year. The only contact she had with people other than her relatives (who lived on the other side of Tokyo and saw her maybe once a month) was when she took the baby for his monthly checkups and could talk to the other mothers there. She was fully absorbed in child care and did not miss her old neighborhood contacts in downtown *(shitamachi)* Tokyo.

We come now to the third stage: the full-house plateau. The woman's child now has his own activities outside the family. During this stage women begin to make friends again, through their children and such groups as the home library movement, children's classes, and children's activities in the neighborhood. In most cases, however, these friends are not as close as school or work friends.

The woman is even more disengaged from her husband's life as he proceeds up the career ladder. He is home less and less, and when he is home he rarely helps. He has long since stopped bringing guests home, and outings are with the whole family. They have for the most part no couples as friends; even when the wives both associate and the husbands both associate, their activities are usually separate. The family at this stage moves closest to the neotraditional model in terms of separation of the worlds of men and women.

This is the point at which the housewife begins to choose neotraditional or new styles of living. She returns to improving her craft as a homemaker and to her own interests. She begins to take advantage of opportunities to study, whether craft or social education. This involvement develops as the children spend more time away from home.

She is now a veteran housewife capable of doing her domestic chores in two to four hours or spending the entire day on housework if she wishes. Even the unwilling mother is now called upon to take her turn as kindergarten mothers' group officer, representative to the local children's group, or PTA officer. Each mother is expected to take her turn at each level of each child's school or at least each level for her youngest child. If she is living in public or company housing, moreover, her turn in the self-governing association will come. In some cases this may involve her in outside activity.[3]

Finally, it is in this stage that the woman makes the decision about working or using her time in other ways. If a home must be purchased, the woman often turns to a part-time job as soon as her children are in middle school. Before this point, piecework at home *(naishoku)* is an alternative. Other women have work, classes, crafts, their own friends, or private pursuits to fill their hours.

All these activities are well within the housewife's role set so long as they are not overdone and the family suffers. In almost every case, however, the housewife related her activities to her housewife's role. (See Fuse 1978, 156–183.) The women with part-time jobs said that they really wanted to take arts and crafts classes but the money was needed to buy a new home or educate the children. The women taking classes in tea ceremony and flower arranging declared these skills would make them better wives. Those involved in adult education argued that the classes would help them to understand their growing children. By way of contrast, all the women involved in volunteer activity for others said they were criticized by neighbors for investing time and energy in activities that brought no benefit to the family. Their neighbors said they must be in a nice position to be able to spend time on such activities, but it would be better if they got a paying part-time job.

During this period, also, the mother must support her children in their schoolwork. If a woman has two children two years apart, she will probably spend a year in the becoming-a-housewife stage, three years in the expanding-circle stage, and then have an eight or nine-year period when both children are in kindergarten through junior high school. Her fourteenth and sixteenth years of marriage are spent with children preparing for high school entrance examinations, and her eighteenth and twentieth years are spent with children preparing for college entrance examinations. Therefore, women in this full-house plateau stage find it important to cultivate a certain number of friends with whom to exchange information about child care and education. Even if they are not interested personally, women accept offices in child-related groups as a duty and to encourage children to study. To maintain these friends and contacts, they engage in activities outside the home ranging from the required PTA to involvement in a number of groups and inviting friends into their homes. The activity level varies with the individual, but the motivations on the structural level clearly reflect the role of child education and the need for related information.

The housewife expects to have outside activities interrupted by events such as a child's entrance examinations or her husband's transfer. Since she must be able to participate in all child-related activities and keep house perfectly, any other activity, whether it be craft classes or a part-time job, must meet the same conditions. It must be done when her family is out, be within bicycling distance of home, allow flexibility in case her children fall ill or there is a school meeting she must attend, and not place too great a burden on the household budget.

Mrs. D is married to a professional pilot, and their annual income is 10 million yen. She pointed out that she was more fortunate than most young mothers in that her closest friends from school lived in her neighborhood. When their children were small the women occasionally gathered at one another's home to chat and discuss child care, but as the children reached the age of two or three and began to take various lessons, the mothers could no longer find a time when they all were free to meet. Now with a four and six-year-old, Mrs. D is waiting until the younger one goes to elementary school so that she can join a study group.

Mrs. E said that although she is now very active in her local community center, this was not the case during the year before her child's high school entrance examinations. She had given up drinking green tea for the whole year to inspire her son, to show him how much she cared, so that he could say as he worked hard, "Mother is giving up one of the things she likes best in life for me, so I too can give up some pleasures and study."

Mrs. F was one of the women I met at a cooking group. The four of us who had comprised a subgroup in the class had agreed to get together occasionally. We were able to do so every two or three months, but this pattern came to an abrupt halt when Mrs. F's daughter entered the last year of junior high school and began studying for her high school entrance examinations. Mrs. F occasionally telephoned to say how much she would like to get together. She asked that we understand her position. Although the children of the three other women were all in upper elementary school or junior high school, our meetings had to take place when school was in session, as the mothers felt they should be at home during school vacations.

We come now to the fourth stage: the shrinking circle. The housewife is now involved in the marriage plans of her children, especially if she has a girl. Women who live in residences they hope to maintain for the rest of their lives indicate the importance of keeping up good relations with neighbors, because investigators come around at the time of their daughters' marriages to ask about the daughters. During this stage the husband's retirement is approaching as well, and this may mean a major change in life-style. Although still young, the couple may have a drastic drop in income. If they live in company housing, they will have to move into something of their own. Even if they do not have to move, they may plan to use the retirement money for a new home or condominium. The woman's life may be uprooted again, and the change in the husband's work hours also affects her life. If the husband begins to disengage from after-work activities, for example, he may begin coming home earlier when he reaches fifty or so. This change reduces the woman's free time, and she has to cut her day shorter to make dinner before he comes home. Moreover, he may be around the house more on weekends. Without children to ask for family outings, either the couple will begin to do things together (such as shopping or sketching) or the woman may feel bound to stay around the house herself to take care of her husband's needs.

Mrs. G had always been active in community improvement. Although she still engages in a few such activities, she has cut back drastically because her husband is now retired and at home. She says he gets bored if she goes out too much and that he is helpless when alone. She also points out that the women in her *danchi*, regardless of age, jokingly refer to their husbands as the "emperor of the house" and say that outside activities have to wait until the man is out and does not need their services.

Mrs. H says that when there were children at home the family always went for drives on Sundays. Now they have sold the car and the two of them sometimes spend their Sundays shopping. Since her husband no longer has business golf on weekends and has no children to take out, he is at a loss as to what to do, so she stays home or goes out with him.

As we can see from the categories described above, the housewife's activity pattern may vary with the stage in her life course. These stages may be interrupted by children's education and husband's retirement, which require that the woman maintain a schedule of flexible activities. Using the average life-course figures given in Figure 1, Table 1 shows a pattern that may be discerned in the life course of the Japanese housewife.

Table 1. Events in the Life Course of the Japanese Housewife

Age	Event
23.1	Marriage
25.3	Birth of first child
27.9	Birth of last child
29	First child enters kindergarten
34.4	Last child enters elementary school
39	First child studying for high school entrance exams
41	Second child studying for high school entrance exams
42	First child studying for college entrance exams
44	Second child studying for college entrance exams
45–46	Last child enters college
50	Last child graduates from college
52–54	Last child's marriage
52	Husband's retirement (at age 55)

Note: Ages are relevant to the housewives studied. By 1980, age at marriage had increased to 25.3 and a small but increasing number of husbands were retiring later than age 55.

Women actively involved outside the home are most likely to come from two age categories. The average housewife has a five-year period from age thirty-four to thirty-nine during which she may engage in a variety of activities by choice or necessity. This is also the peak PTA period, and the time she will be called upon to help with child-related activities. Then, between age forty-five and fifty-two or so, she will have another such period, interrupted only by her children's marriages. These interruptions are expected by housewives in every stage of the life course and determine how they will use their time during the relatively free periods.

In comparison with her American counterpart, then, the Japanese housewife faces more regularly scheduled interruptions of outside activity. The American woman can, at least in theory, expand her participation in the work world (or in any other activity) and continue that activity without interruption when her children enter school. Also, at least in theory, she can expect that, provided she has the skills, she can find full-time employment. The Japanese housewife, in contrast, must not only contend with early age limits and the availability of only temporary or part-time positions in many fields but must also deal with extended interruptions of any activity in which she might engage. And, finally, an early retirement age for her husband brings accompanying changes in their life-style.

The life-course stages of the sample for this study are given in Table 2. In the case of the interviewees I was able to ascertain more clearly how they fell into the four stages. In the case of survey respondents,

Table 2. Life-Course Stages of Respondents

In-Depth Interviewees		*Survey Respondents*	
Stage	*Number of Women*	*Age of Children Present*	*Number of Women*
Becoming a housewife	1	No children	21
Expanding circle	2	Plan more children	31
Full-house plateau	42	Preschool	79
Shrinking circle	5	Elementary school	80
		Junior high and	
		high school	53
		College	26
		Grown	51

however, I used the presence of children of certain age groups to explore activity in terms of the life course. The presence of younger children would be the decisive factor in placing a woman in the various stages.

Since a few women cannot have children, their life course is different from that of the average housewife. Although I do not deal here with childless women in detail, my impressions are that they tend to keep their job or engage in part-time work or study throughout their life. These women appear to spend more time with their husbands than do women with children. Thus they may be able to avoid some of the readjustment problems that occur when the average housewife's husband retires.

Work and the Life Course

Newspapers, magazines, and television all show a great deal of interest in the working woman—from what to wear to the office to labor legislation improving the working conditions for women in Japan. The popular media generally portray the married woman at home with the children or looking after the house. This image blurs, however, when we compare it with the statistical data on women and work. Changes are taking place in the composition of the female labor force.

At the time of this study, 45.8 percent of women aged fifteen and above were in the labor force and comprised 37.4 percent of the entire labor force.[4] Whereas in 1960 some 62.4 percent of the women in the labor force were unmarried, in 1976 unmarried women accounted for only 35.8 percent of the female labor force. The age composition of the female labor force is also changing. In 1976, women over the age of forty represented 34.7 percent of the female labor force, in contrast to 19 percent in 1960. Furthermore, during the 1965–1973 period the number of persons engaged in piecework at home, the majority of whom are housewives, increased two and one-half times. The M-shaped curve representing the labor-force participation of women peaks at the twenties and forties.[5] One would expect to find women less involved in the labor force during the expanding-circle and early full-house plateau stages.

A final factor for consideration is the type of work the women do. *Naishoku,* piecework at home, might be done over the entire life course. Payment for such work—for example, assembling machinery parts or sewing parts of garments—can be as low as a few yen per item completed.[6] In 1973, some 13.9 percent of the women surveyed doing this type of work said they did it because they had free time. This response fell to 9.1 percent in 1978. The leading reasons for such work were clearly financial need: 41 percent worked to support the family budget, and 29.3 percent did it because they could not work outside the home. This type of work, unless it can be done in a group, certainly limits the time the housewife has to socialize with her neighbors, much less to participate in civic or leisure groups. Since the average wage computed on an hourly basis for this type of work was 262 yen and the average monthly income was 25,000 yen, the net gain to the housewife was very low.

Participating in a family business is a second type of work that might be combined with home responsibilities when children are small. A third type is temporary or part-time work. When I first arrived in Tokyo in 1967, most shopping for daily necessities was done at little specialized shops in the neighborhood. Today, in almost every neighborhood one can find supermarkets side by side with the small shops. In these supermarkets or chain stores one finds not only young women but middle-aged women working at cash registers and marking stock. A cursory look at the posters indicating job openings reveals that they are recruiting neighborhood housewives, and so much the better if the supermarket is located within a *danchi* and the wives can work in their own residential complex. Hours are fairly flexible, and the peak hours are times when most women would be out shopping anyway.

In the supermarket near my home, the women at the cash registers seem to come primarily from the *danchi* and know most of the women shoppers. Because they work in jobs close to their homes, their children often drop in on the way home from school to say they have returned or ask for spending money. The hourly wages for such work ranged from 300 to 400 yen. Such stores, then, provide an outlet for housewives who want to work but not too far from home.

Not only a housewife's life course but also her life-style may be expected to play a part in her participation in the labor force. A housewife whose husband is highly educated and employed in nonmanual work is more likely to concentrate full time on home and family. If the husband is less educated and does manual work, he is more likely to expect the wife to engage in work of some kind. (See Iga 1978, 55ff.)

The great majority of women I surveyed in Santama City worked before marriage; only 14 percent did not. Younger women were more likely than older ones to have worked before marriage. Whereas employment in a company or with the government was by far the largest category of work, older women (over forty-five) had higher rates of *naishoku* and family business experience before marriage than younger women, and women with higher educations and younger women had higher rates of professional experience. Women who worked before marriage had a slightly higher propensity to be working at present. (Some 37.9 percent of these women were working at present in contrast to 28.3 percent of women who did not work before marriage.)

Becoming a Housewife

What happens when these women marry? Do they work during the becoming-a-housewife stage? Fifty percent of those surveyed did not work after marriage even before the first child was born. And if a woman did not work then, she was less likely ever to work in a family business, manage her own business, or work in a profession than she was to work only part-time or not at all. Women married to blue-collar workers had the highest rate (58.8 percent) of continuing work until a child was born. This finding supports the suggestion that women whose husbands are engaged in manual work may be less able to concentrate their energies fully on the home.

Whether a woman continues to work and the type of work she does are related to her education. The percentage of women not working in the becoming-a-housewife stage increased from 43.9 percent for those with only compulsory education to 62.5 percent for women with university education. Of those engaged in *naishoku* during this stage, 75 percent had completed only compulsory education, in contrast to the 69.3 percent of those continuing in professions who had a junior college or university education. Lastly, the percentage of those working during this stage increased with the age of the respondent—ranging from 40.4 percent for women thirty-five and under to 62.1 percent for those over forty-five.

Mrs. I is a junior high school graduate whose husband is a sewage construction and repair man. Their annual income is about 1.8 million yen. She had worked seven years in a coffee shop before her marriage. She agreed to marry on the condition that she would not have to work, a condition her friends advised her to set. They told her that if a woman works, the husband just drinks up the extra money and thinks less seriously of his responsibility to his family. Now the mother of a second grader, she thinks it is very important to stay home until her son graduates from high school, but eventually she wants to own a snack bar or coffee shop to provide income in her old age. She is glad she did not work during the early stages of her marriage even though they have a fairly unstable income (her husband is paid by the job) and can never hope to own their own home.

Mrs. J has been married six years and has no children. Her husband works for a large trading company, and their annual income is about 3.5 million yen. She had worked as a guide at Expo '70 and then for an airline as a reservation clerk until her marriage. She had expected to continue working, but her husband was transferred to Tokyo. Now she teaches English conversation part time to children in their homes. She thinks women should work because it makes them feel part of society and teaches them to be more understanding toward their working husbands. They should not work, though, unless they can get the housework done first. Mrs. J herself would only work if she had spare time after she did her housework.

Mrs. K is a registered nurse who continued to work during the becoming-a-housewife stage and stopped with the birth of her son, now five years old. Her husband, a salesman for a publishing company, has an annual income of about 3.5 million yen. She wants to return to work when her son is in school, but she worries about her ability to do so. Working was difficult even before he was born because her husband never did anything to help. She said this lack of help put quite a strain on her.

A husband's failure to pitch in with domestic duties is a common reason for a woman not to continue to work after marriage. Most of the women I interviewed indicated that they did not receive or expect any help from their husband. This sample included full-time housewives with professional qualifications such as pharmacists or teachers as well as women who continued to work in their family shops. (The few women whose husbands did help were exceptions. For example, one was Christian and active in church affairs; one was an American-born Japanese who returned to Japan after World War II; one was active in the union at his place of work; and still another was a freelance photographer and home more than the average husband.) Even those women who worked indicated they accepted the home as their responsibility. While they did not mind if husbands put away *futon* (bedding) in the morning or ran an occasional errand in the neighborhood, they would not be happy if the husband were seen running the vacuum cleaner or doing the laundry.[7] Moreover, they did not want their husbands to accuse them of neglecting their duties as housewives. Such women, then, took on two jobs—the home and their work outside it.

Expanding Circle and Early Full-House Plateau

The majority of those surveyed did not work after the birth of their first child (60.1 percent). Of those who did continue to work, 19.4 percent were engaged in the family business, 22.2 percent in *naishoku,* and 13.9 percent in part-time work. Women in other types of work, especially professionals, those in family businesses, and full-time employees, were much more likely to have continued even though they had a child. In other words, those currently engaged in full-time work tended to continue in spite of life-course changes. But the majority of women, currently either not working or employed part-time, left the labor force with the change in life course.

Women with higher education are less likely to work after a child is born than those with compulsory education only. The latter, moreover, have a *naishoku* rate that is several times that of the former (26.8 percent versus 4.3 percent for university graduates). With the single exception of those whose husbands were self-employed, regardless of husband's occupation the majority of wives did not work after the birth of their first child. The wives of self-employed men tended to engage in either *naishoku* or the family business. The stage in the life course is more important than husband's occupation in women's employment outside the home. In terms of employment within the home, however, women married to blue-collar workers had the highest rate. This finding supports the earlier suggestion that such women are not able to devote their energies entirely to the home.

Mrs. L is married to a university lecturer whose annual income is about 3 million yen. She worked in a university office even after the birth of her first child, putting the child in government-run day care. When the second child was unable to get into such a facility she resigned her job, but she wishes she could return to work. She says that she probably would have quit work anyway when her children entered grade school, because the after-school day care center would have sent the children home at five and they would have had to walk through a lonely area in the dark in winter. If Mrs. L could get a full-time job in the future, however, she would like to work.

Mrs. M is married to a grocer and works in the shop. She hopes that when the children get older she can arrange to take a holiday once a week and join a women's group or class of some sort. Now her children are in day care while she works in the shop. Since she has to manage all the cooking and cleaning at home as well as her work, her days are completely filled.

Mrs. N, a nursery school teacher before she married a university professor, believes strongly that a woman should not work when there are children in the home. She feels her training can be put to good use on her own children; she would not leave them to go out and work.

Mrs. O, however, who was divorced, worked as a nursery school teacher until her daughter was nine. She enjoyed the work, but she feels that now, at forty, she is too old to keep up with little children. She also wanted to take care of her own child. She misses the money she earned and has had to cut back on her activities. She has channeled her energies into a children's theater group. She is now remarried and her husband, who works in a bread factory, makes about 2 million yen a year.

Apart from the difficulties of arranging for child care, there is social pressure on women to stay home. Mrs. P, a nursery school teacher who quit at the birth of her first child but went back to work within the year, told of the pressures placed on her by coresidents in her apartment house, who criticized her for putting her son in day care. An advocate of day care as a means of making children independent, she campaigned in her apartment house to make the women realize that such facilities were not just social welfare or charity institutions for the economically deprived. This woman has an advantage in that her husband works in the city office and can come home in the early evening to watch the children when she has a professional meeting.

Full-House Plateau and Shrinking Circle

Who, then, are the women working now?[8] The proportion increases with the age of the housewife, reflecting the second peak of the M-

Table 3. Women Now Working by Age of Respondent

Age	Working	Not Working	DK/NA	Number
35 and under	26.8%	71.0%	2.2%	93
36–45	35.4	63.1	1.5	65
Over 45	44.2	52.9	2.9	70

curve. (See Table 3.) The proportion of women with compulsory education now working (60.5 percent) is almost double that of women who have completed at least high school (31.4 percent). The former, however, tend to be engaged in *naishoku* or family business. Women's labor-force participation also varies inversely with their husband's education (26 percent for wives of university-educated men versus 61.5 percent for those whose husbands have only compulsory education). This finding is also reflected in the lower percentages of wives of white-collar and professional men who were currently working (20.5 percent) in comparison to wives of blue-collar workers (40.4 percent) or self-employed men (62.5 percent).

In terms of life-course stage, the proportion of women surveyed who were currently working increases from 29.2 percent of those with preschool children to 51 percent of those with grown children. The highest rate of full-time employment (9.8 percent) was among women with grown children. Women in stem families had a higher tendency (48.8 percent) to be working than those in nuclear families (31.2 percent). This finding may reflect the greater mobility of a woman who has someone to look after the children. For those who do work when they have small children, *naishoku* is the most popular choice (equal to family business). Yet even this type of work is hard to manage.

Mrs. Q is married to a microfilm photographer whose annual income is about 3 million yen. She greeted me in a room filled with boxes of men's socks. Part of a chain assembly system, she must sew price tags on the socks and pass them on to the next person, who puts them in plastic bags. A truck delivers and picks up her consignment. Since her husband opposes this work, she keeps it a secret from him. Although she could not say how much time she actually puts into the work (sometimes all day, but sometimes not at all for two or three days), she earns 30,000 yen a month. The work is hard to manage—

the quantity of socks is so great (a two-day consignment amounted to three or four waist-high piles of socks) that Mrs. Q must ask a friend to help when she is busy with PTA activities. She pays the friend and buys cake for them to eat while working. Then she has to put away the socks before her husband comes home. Since he usually comes home very late at night, she manages to hide the socks in the cupboards when she gets out the bedding.

Mrs. R is married to an engineer who earns about 3.5 million yen a year. She assembles machinery parts, for which she earns about 1.5 million yen a year. She uses a machine furnished by the consigner; once she hurt her hand on the machine and was unable to work for two months. She works every morning from 8:30 to 10:00; then she hangs out laundry and gets lunch for her children (three years old and twenty months). She works another hour in the afternoon while the children nap. Since the machinery is noisy she cannot work at night for fear of bothering the neighbors, and she never works when her husband is home because he does not like it. She is saving the money to use for lessons for herself when the children are in school. She has tried other things, such as selling Tupperware, in order to get her children in day care. There were no vacancies, however, so she resigned herself to *naishoku*.

Mrs. S, a pricer in a supermarket, is married to a blue-collar worker, and their combined income is 3.5 million yen a year. She indicated quite clearly the conditions under which a mother of school-aged children may work. The workplace must be close enough to walk or bicycle to, because public transportation would cut into earnings; the hours have to flexible, so that a mother can attend PTA and take care of sick children; and the workday must allow her to be home to fix dinner before her husband returns.

Unemployed women were asked why they were not working. The presence of small children (32.4 percent) and domestic chores (26.8 percent) were the most frequently mentioned reasons, followed by "don't want to" (12.0 percent) and illness or other family circumstances (12.7 percent). The presence of small children was the major reason given by younger women for not working, whereas women over thirty-five most frequently indicated they were busy at home. Women over thirty-five were more likely not to want to work than younger women, but they also had a higher tendency to want to work and be unable to find a suitable job.

No one in a stem family indicated that she wanted to work but could not find a suitable job, whereas 8.8 percent of the women in nuclear families faced this problem. Members of stem families who were not working were three times more likely to indicate they did not want to work than members of nuclear families. In the stem family, there is someone at home to look after the children during the day or after school.

Will these women work in the future? Some 45 percent said yes—10.6 percent full time and 34.4 percent part time. Younger women were more likely to plan to work in the future than older women (55.8 percent for those thirty-five and under, 45.5 percent for those thirty-six to forty-five, and 25.6 percent for those over forty-five). Non-working women whose husbands were self-employed were more likely not to intend to work in the future (71.4 percent); 40 to 50 percent of women married to men in other types of jobs did intend to work.

Those who said they wanted to work now but could not find suitable employment had the highest aspirations to return to full-time work (30 percent). The majority of women not working because of small children also expected to work in the future, whereas those who were not working because they did not want to or because they were busy at home or faced family opposition were most likely not to plan to work in the future.

From the standpoint of life course, only among women with grown children did a majority indicate they did not expect to work in the future. Since this is the stage during which the highest percentage of women surveyed were actually working, one might assume that those who wanted to work were already doing so. In earlier stages, more than 50 percent of the women expected to return to work; mothers of small children had the greatest tendency to expect to work full time in the future.

Work does vary with life-course stage, although this factor alone does not explain why women are or are not working. Mrs. T, a woman very active in the home library movement, spends several days a week at a city library. When asked why she did not take a paying job at the library, she replied: "Oh, no, if I worked I'd have responsibility. I'd have to go even if I didn't want to. If I'm a volunteer I can stay home when my children are ill or when I don't want to go." Mrs. U, whose husband works in a research institute and earns 5.5 million yen a year, hopes someday to find a job as a part-time English teacher. She stated: "If it's for money, I don't want to work. If there is something interesting to do, however, of course I want to work." The woman who worked as a supermarket pricer indicated that she would rather attend various classes than work.

Women who were able to engage in fulfilling or creative work, such as teaching arts and crafts, indicated that this work was their secondary purpose in life—after home and family. Women with skills, such as one former draftsman, said they wanted to return to their fields in the future. The differences lie in whether the women see themselves as returning to work because they have to for economic reasons or whether they have a choice. Obviously the women who said they did not want the responsibility or would not work just for the money were not in financial distress. Women in the position of the pricer, however, could not afford to answer this way.

Yet even when a second income is very much needed, women try to stay home when there are small children. One reason is the lack of child-care facilities, but another is the strong feeling that their small children need them at home. For mothers of school-aged children, reasons for not working vary with economic circumstances, skills, and the woman's desire for work and her interpretation of the job market. As one interviewee put it: "Society should provide a way for women to engage in permanent skilled or professional part-time employment so they can make use of their skills, contribute to society, and still take care of their responsibilities at home. Not only does the present system make it hard for women to use their talents, but it is a loss to society as well."

Generational Differences

While most housewives might be expected to follow the stages of the life course as outlined above, the life histories of women in different generations may differ. How do the women interpret generational differences?

One aspect of change is that of child care. Mothers of junior high school students who were active in the community center told me that when they were younger a mother would never ask someone to look after her children, but now younger women take turns looking after one another's children while they attend classes. These active women thought that this was a very positive change. In contrast, women trying to arrange for child care at city facilities told me that older people, especially men, who decided resource allocations for such facilities could not understand why young mothers needed them. If the older generation had looked after its children, the younger women could do so too. They were accused of shirking their duties as mothers.

Senior citizens at the community center were also aware of generational differences. Those living with their married children pointed out that the brides were no longer interested in what older women could teach them. Even in the preparation of traditional food, the brides preferred to use cookbooks or television rather than ask grandmother. Older people's ideas were said to be out of date, and they felt they did not have a role in life. In most cases they had moved into a new home, either their son's home or one they had built together with the young couple, and the bride was the housewife in charge. These women were worried about a permissive approach to child care and recalled the "good old days" when children had to do chores around the house.

Active older or middle-aged women also had opinions on the changing generations. Mrs. V, vice president of her regional women's organization,[9] points out that when she was young this was the key organization. People were concerned with their neighborhood relationships, and although not everyone was active in the regional group, more people showed interest than now. Younger women these days are very active in the PTA and also have a variety of "circle" activities to choose from. They are not interested in the regional women's group. With a proliferation of activities for younger women, a wider variety of life-styles can be expected.

Mrs. W, a fifty-year-old woman in charge of the women's auxiliary of a progressive political party, says that active women in the postwar generation knew that political activity is essential to getting anything done. In the current generation, however, women are afraid of political activity and prefer to engage in nonpartisan consumer movements. She feels these women do not understand the realities of the situation and that their ways of dealing with problems are weak. Her group recruits members who have been active since the war. Younger women who join tend to be long-term residents of the area and have a high school education, in contrast to the college education of most older women. Mrs. W fears that younger people are not as civic-minded as older women. Younger women are in fact much more mobile, moving in and out of temporary rented housing as their husbands are transferred around. This mobility may be reflected in a lowered interest in local activities.

Housing and the Life Course

The formation of informal groups is affected by home ownership and permanency in the neighborhood, as well as by the housing itself—proximity, orientation, and visibility of neighbors. (See Festinger et al. 1950.) Related influences include the presence of public halls in housing complexes and the location of such focal points as the road to school, the bus stop, or the shopping center. Lastly, there is the question of whether the residence itself can provide a sense of identity. As William Michelson (1974, 155) indicates, what people perceive in their environment has a considerable effect on their behavior, but at the same time the environment must create sufficient opportunity for a certain perception to develop. For example, limiting housing to employees of a certain company or to people with certain levels of income may create a sense of identity, as can the presence of a high-rise complex in the midst of a neighborhood of single-family homes. In Japan, two types of housing milieu in particular have this effect: company housing and the *danchi*.

Companies expecting to transfer a significant proportion of their staff often find it feasible to build or rent company housing. Residence in such housing tends to produce a homogeneous population of temporary residents that is distinguished from the neighborhood at large by their common workplace and the expectation that their stay will be of short duration. For housewives, the instability may affect long-term involvement. Moreover, while homogeneity may make it easier for them to integrate into their own housing milieu, it may also hamper their activities. A woman may know too much about another's family situation, for example, and gossip might lead to bad relations even among husbands. (See Vogel 1967, 106n.) Questions of company status of husbands may create "vertical relations" among the women. (See Kunitachi 1977, 46.) Or, to take an extreme example, the visibility of a wife's comings and goings in such housing can either inhibit her activities or oblige her to sneak out to avoid disapproval. As Sonya Salamon (1975, 160) indicates, "in Japanese company housing, neighbors not only have this kind . . . of access to knowledge, but they also have access to other private and vital information such as salary. The women are probably right in their assessment that it is not a good idea to become too friendly with their neighbors."

Danchi were originally constructed to provide temporary housing after World War II but in fact people tend to stay in them for a longer period of time. Some families have spent their entire lives there, and the second *danchi* generation has grown, married, and may be living in *danchi* of their own. (See Ōyabu 1975a and 1975b.) The distinctive construction of the *danchi* (usually a high-rise with a number of similar buildings in one compound) contrasts sharply with the private residences and shops around them. In older neighborhoods, the influx of a new group of people living in distinctive housing frequently results in divisions. *Danchi* residents (often called the *danchi zoku,* or "*danchi* tribe"), as newcomers, are not always accepted by the older residents; in extreme cases, they form completely separate interest groups in conflict with one another.

Residents of the Japan Housing Corporation's *danchi* have, in particular, been characterized as a fairly homogeneous group. They tend to have higher than average incomes, are employed by large industries in white-collar occupations, are college graduates, and enter the *danchi* when men are between the ages of twenty-five and forty and women are between twenty and thirty.[10] This homogeneity might be expected to promote interaction among residents, but it seems to have the opposite effect. The lack of a structure from which leaders can be identified, and the lack of residents who enter a *danchi* expecting to live there a long time, can inhibit the growth of *danchi* organizations. (See Kiefer 1968, chap. 5.)

There are two arguments about *danchi* wives' participation in various activities. Christie Kiefer (1968, 38) suggests that the lack of clearly defined lines of authority in the *danchi* gives wives a chance to become more involved in "task-oriented civic organizations." Morioka Kiyomi, however, found that involvement tends to be in hobby, study, and occasionally religious activities rather than in civic tasks. A Ministry of Education study ("Danchi no Josei wa Iyoku Tappuri" 1978) concluded that women living in *danchi* have a greater than average participation rate in activities outside the home, as well as a greater desire to participate in such activities in the future, but the activities described did not involve civic participation such as volunteer or consumer activity.

One aspect of *danchi* living that differentiates it from company housing is the ability to remain anonymous if one so chooses. The *danchi* provides a milieu in which there are usually no husband-related ties to consider or any intention of permanently remaining in the area. It is possible, therefore, to choose activities freely or to remain anonymous. On the other hand, the independent home surrounded by walls offers more privacy than the *danchi*. Since the *danchi* veranda tends to become a showplace for the family laundry and bedding there results a kind of competition about the quality of bedding and the like. (See Kiefer 1968, 35, 92.) Women may therefore wish to conceal whatever they can, denying others entrance into their apartments. In other words, social interaction within the *danchi* may often take place outside the individual residences. Thus the physical layout of stairwells, green space, and common meeting facilities becomes very important in preserving privacy in a *danchi* complex.

Contrary to the picture of isolated, lonely people living in boxlike apartments, the *danchi* can become the locus of personal relations and the exchange of services such as babysitting, borrowing, and lending. Ōyabu Jūichi (1975b) argues that as a second generation of *danchi* dwellers returns to the parents' *danchi* to say hello not only to parents but to neighbors, they come to think of the *danchi* as home. Thus even without home ownership the kinds of solidarity suggested by Irokawa Daikichi (1975) may be expected.

The histories of the women I interviewed show how housing differences influence their activity patterns. In the sample survey, residents of company housing (7.9 percent), rented apartments (18.4 percent), and owned condominiums (1.3 percent) tend to be younger than those living in *danchi* (8.8 percent) and privately owned homes (56.6 percent). Family incomes of those in their own homes or condominiums tend to be higher than those in other categories. The majority of company housing and condominium residents and the highest proportion of homeowners are in white-collar occupations. Blue-collar workers account for a lower proportion of homeowners than renters. Husbands in *danchi* and apartments have less education than those in other categories, as do wives in company housing and *danchi*.

The women surveyed are a mobile group: 63 percent have lived in a different type of residence in the past. Those in their own homes and those in *danchi* (82.5 percent and 57.9 percent, respectively) are most likely to want to stay put. Others intend to move primarily in order to live in a larger residence or to own their own home. In contrast to the nuclear-family sample in company housing, apartments, and condominiums, 15 percent of *danchi* dwellers and 28.7 percent of homeowners are stem families. Difficulties of space and a sense of impermanence may stand in the way of stem-family living in an apartment or company housing, whereas the higher percentage of stem families among home dwellers might be accounted for by the pooling of the resources of the two generations.

With the exception of persons living in their own homes, the great majority have lived less than five years in their present dwellings. Perhaps most striking is the increase in percentage of families living in their own homes as they move along the life course.[11] Now let us take a closer look at what the residents of the various housing milieus say about themselves.

Apartment Dwellers

It was difficult to meet such women for interviews. Trying various types of classes, activities, or friends of friends at the community center and other places did not work. Neither did asking the majority of my interviewees. Not even the PTA could introduce me to a woman who lived in an apartment. Finally, I located some apartment dwellers through a woman who distributed educational material for the city and thus knew all the residents of her area. I reached another group through the efforts of a cooking teacher I interviewed. The apartment women I interviewed, like those surveyed, had less education than other categories (three compulsory education, five high school, and two above). Two were married to shopkeepers. Their annual income was the lowest of any housing category (mean 3.2 million yen), but they paid the highest rent (mean 26,000 yen).

With the exception of the shopkeepers, who intended to stay put because of their work and inability to buy a home, the majority planned to move as soon as they could raise the funds—either to return to the country or to move in with parents in Tokyo. In terms of the life course, one is becoming a housewife, one is in the expanding-circle stage, and the other eight are at the full-house plateau, all with elementary or preschool children. With the exception of the two shopkeepers' wives, only one woman worked (cleaning the public bath and serving as the superintendent of her apartment building).

All of these women indicated a lack of communication with neighbors. They were either unable (lacking time in the case of the shopkeepers' wives and lacking money in the others) or not interested in community activities or classes. They felt transient and unable to comprehend the notion of community or recognize opportunities for group participation or making friends. They saw themselves as isolated but did not necessarily want to get involved with their neighborhood residents. As one put it: "I just want to avoid trouble. Trouble? Oh it usually starts over comparing what we own or buy. I just don't like that, so I avoid getting close to people." Not one of these women indicated that she had made friends through PTA or was active in PTA beyond compulsory attendance.

Unfortunately, the strong correlation between lower education and apartment living in the sample does not allow these variables to be separated. In their own eyes and the eyes of other housewives, however, these women are the most isolated group—an unknown group of women living in what the nonapartment dwellers classify as relatively expensive and not very nice housing. They see themselves as unable to compete with women living in their own homes in terms of possessions; furthermore, they are reluctant to put much energy into decorating a residence they hope to leave. They say that women living in their own homes are different than they are, and they clearly recognize this as a difference in status. They are unwilling to join PTA and groups that might bring other women into their homes.

Danchi Women

"When we first moved into this *danchi* [thirty years ago] we all liked the idea of privacy. We did not want the old, sticky type of relationships. But after a while we got lonesome."

"Of course I say hello to women on my stairwell, but I don't go so far as to invite them in."

The *danchi* women I interviewed include a variety of types. They ranged from one with only compulsory education to five high school graduates and four with even more education. Their ages ranged from the late twenties (one) through the thirties (seven), and two respondents were over fifty. Rents clustered around 10,000 yen a month, and incomes ranged from 1.8 to 6 million yen per year (mean 3.6 million yen per year). Only one woman worked, teaching flower arrangement and helping out at kimono sales as well as doing light cleaning for an

American woman in her neighborhood. All except the two over fifty were in the full-house plateau stage.

Danchi life is the subject of a great deal of speculation by non-*danchi* residents. Women who lived in their own homes told me of rumors about arguments among *danchi* neighbors and how difficult it must be to live in cramped quarters. On the other hand, they assured me that they had friends who lived in *danchi* and that their children played with *danchi* children. When I asked them to tell me how many friends they had among *danchi* women and how they had met, however, almost none could name such a friend. They assured me that their children must know someone in a *danchi* because *danchi* children went to the neighborhood school, or they told me that surely someone in their PTA-related group is from a *danchi*. Once again, however, most of them had never visited anyone living in a *danchi*.

Danchi residents explained that their quarters are too cramped to invite in women who live in their own "big" homes. They were very sensitive to this difference. One woman said she had invited PTA friends home once but they had suggested instead that they meet in the larger home of another member. Nor do *danchi* women necessarily form friendships within the *danchi* itself. Bringing in *danchi* neighbors would reduce their privacy, and they strive to avoid "trouble" with neighbors. Friendships formed in the *danchi* are inevitably with persons who live either in separate buildings or on different floors. In other words, space is needed as a buffer zone to preserve privacy. These women expressed interest in "circle" activity within the *danchi* if there were a public hall for such events, but not if it meant inviting people into their homes. An older woman pointed out that young women are not interested in civic service; everything is centered around their own homes and families.

The desire to own a place of one's own plays a role in the activities chosen by *danchi* wives. A city official familiar with patterns of women's participation in local activities pointed out that it is not the nearby *danchi* women who make use of the facility but rather women in their own homes who live farther away. *Danchi* women "prefer to work." A woman (living in her own home) long active in civic affairs said that unless a woman is living in her own home she does not have the reserves *(yoyū)* to engage in volunteer and other activities. Women not in their own homes are unsettled and cannot think beyond the needs of their own families.

Although most of the *danchi* women I interviewed do not work, they do not seem to have the means necessary even to improve their present lot in life. With the exception of the apartment of the one woman who worked, the *danchi* I visited were depressing in the extreme. Even women who had lived in their *danchi* for more than ten years made no effort to make the apartments cheery. Many had torn *fusuma* (paper sliding doors) patched with newspaper. Gummed paper for repairing these doors is certainly available in supermarkets, but these women seemed lethargic about improving their situation. Many could have improved things by clearing out the stacks of newspapers and magazines in their apartments. The apartment of the working woman, in contrast, was brightly decorated with curtains and potted geraniums. Things were neat and inviting but not costly.

The primary activities of the *danchi* women I interviewed were related to children's school or religion. (Several attended meetings of one of the evangelical New Religions.) These women had few real friends in either the *danchi* or the neighborhood at large. Occasionally they invited other *danchi* women in for tea, but usually they confined themselves to talking in the *danchi* compound or on the stairs.

Living in a housing complex seems to set up barriers between coresidents. All wanted to avoid "trouble"—getting into fights over children's differences or as the result of rumors spread about one of the residents. Younger women told me they were surprised when they moved into the *danchi* that older residents asked about everything, even their husband's income. Certainly the poor construction of *danchi* contributes to the privacy problem and some of the rumors. In one *danchi,* residents on lower floors could hear water coming down the pipes from the apartments above and wanted to prohibit bathing and even flushing the toilet after 10 PM. When residents on the upper floors pointed out that many husbands would never be able to take a bath, the idea was dropped, but residents on the upper floors were careful not to flush the toilet too often at night. Another example of the strains that can develop is the case of the carpet washer. One *danchi* resident had washed her carpet in the yard using one of the outside faucets. Since each household shares the water bill and not every household has a carpet to wash, the residents' association decided that no one would be allowed to wash carpets or other large items such as cars using the outside faucet. A third example of trouble concerned rumors about the financial insecurity of one of the families. When the family heard the rumors they realized that they were based on a private discussion held in the bathroom where the children could not hear. The conversation had carried through the thin bathroom walls to their neighbor's ears and thence to others!

Thus *danchi* women see themselves as separate from the women living in private homes, yet they are unable to form a community among themselves. Unlike women in apartments, however, they often form casual friendships within their complexes. Nevertheless, they tend not to allow even other *danchi* dwellers into their lives and they try to preserve anonymity. This pattern presents a very different situation from women in company housing.

Women in Company Housing

"As soon as a woman moves into a *shataku* (company housing), she starts planning to move out." "I go out to get away from the other women in the *shataku* and avoid trouble." "When I was young and living in the *shataku,* it was very enjoyable. We all were friends and went back and forth with our children. I'm glad that I never got involved in *shataku* trouble."

Interviewees in company housing had a fairly high level of education—four were high school graduates and six had attended junior college and above. They were young (eight in their thirties and two in their forties), and all were in the full-house plateau stage. Family incomes ranged from 2.5 million to 5.7 million yen per year (mean 3.8 million yen). Rents were the lowest of any, ranging from 3,500 yen per month to 16,300 yen (in the latter case a fixed percentage of the husband's income). Mean rent was 6,940 yen per month. Three wives worked part-time. (One tutored junior high school students, one worked as a pharmacist twice a week, and one was employed as a pricer in a supermarket.) These three were also active in other pursuits, including consumer affairs, the home library movement, the community center, PTA, and study activity. One woman did *naishoku* but was not active otherwise.

Women in company housing informed me that they avoided getting too close to women in the same housing complex because "trouble" (usually, as in the *danchi,* related to children or rumors) could affect their husbands and because they might find themselves living with some of the same neighbors again in the future. It would be terrible, they told me, if they made an enemy of a person who preceded them to their next place of residence. In such a case, their new environment would be prejudiced against them before they arrived. They also knew when one another's husbands entered the company and had learned to predict income very accurately. One woman observed: "The income may be the same, but some women spend it one way and some another; some save it and some just throw it away."

To avoid the possibility of "trouble," several women indicated that they had deliberately tried to find friends outside company housing. One, for example, joined a table tennis class and did basket weaving. Furthermore, women who had tried to form groups in company housing found that too much activity might be criticized by others and come back to their husbands, so they broadened their sphere of activity to outside company housing. One woman said that her home library activities are considered "pink" (politically radical) by some of the company housing residents. She also said that when they moved there from a *danchi,* her husband told her not to ask any of the wives to babysit because those above her in status could not be asked to perform such favors while those below her would have difficulty refusing.

Finally, many women in company housing indicated their constant uncertainty about being transferred and said they had moved frequently. Such women are therefore reluctant to seek outside work (unless they have specific skills such as tutoring or are interested in *naishoku* or the like). Of course, there are usually part-time jobs such as the pricer's in the supermarket, but women expecting to move at any moment indicated they always put off looking for work. Once they move, they are busy orienting themselves to their new situation and finding out about schools and so forth. Meeting local people through activities provides them with a quick source of local information.

Women in Their Own Homes and Condominiums

The condominium residents I interviewed were highly educated (four high school graduates and five who attended junior college and above). They were for the most part in the full-house plateau stage (six women); one was childless and two were in the shrinking-circle stage. Their family income—the highest mean family income of any category (6.1 million yen a year)—ranged from 3.5 million to 8 million yen per year. Two women worked, one as an English conversation teacher and the other as a kindergarten teacher.

Women in their own homes were highly educated, as well. (Nine out of ten had a junior college education or above.) Nine were in the full-house plateau stage and one was in the shrinking-circle stage. Annual family incomes ranged from 2.5 to 10 million yen (mean 4.3 million yen). Only one worked, as an *ikebana* teacher, but several of the younger women said they would like to work part time at some interesting job when their children were older.

These women did not really need to work and were only interested if the job was appealing—as more than one woman said, "not merely for money." Their activity outside the home was correlated with their free time and high education. For the sake of their children, they were more likely to be concerned about their neighborhood relations than were women in the other housing categories (with the exception of a few *danchi* women who expected to stay there all their lives). If their children wished to stay in their house in the future, it would not do to have bad relations with neighbors.

Women in these categories tended to get involved in the home library movement or volunteer work. Older women who had just moved into a condominium were motivated by a desire to make friends, but younger women's motives were more likely related to their children. They tended to develop friends from their child's kindergarten and keep these friends if they shared common interests. Such women participated in "circle" activities together or formed their own reading or study group to have a reason to meet. These groups served a variety of functions for them: making new friends, gathering information related to child care and other role activities, and preserving long-term friendships. The women tended to stay in crafts and study groups (rather than those corresponding to the life course) for a long time and to maintain friendships over the years.

Women living in houses rather than condominiums seemed more settled. Two types of women lived in the condominiums: younger women planning to raise their completed families and older women who had moved there after living in a series of company houses, *danchi,* or whatever. The two groups were very different. The younger women did not regard themselves as permanent residents; the older women did. The younger women expected to make friends in the condominium and neighborhood through their children, but the older women did not know how to go about finding friends their own age. They also told me that they perceived the condominium as "young" and had little contact with younger women.

Even though one might expect that higher visibility within a condominium (as compared to a private house) would lead older women to seek one another out, this does not happen unless the two women's "daily rhythm is the same." If two older women take out the garbage at the same time, for example the condominium stairs may serve as a place of contact. Merely living in the same complex does not seem to be enough, however. The younger women, by contrast, spend more time in the public spaces because of their children and are therefore more likely to meet one another. Both groups, however, had an unsettled quality. Even when they knew they were permanent, the older women told me they would really like a place with a bit of a garden. The younger women all expected to move.

All condominium women saw their condominium as a unit. They spoke of activities for children or classes for wives there and mentioned the mood within the condominium, indicating whether it was friendly or not. One older woman, a cooking teacher, discussed the loneliness of the older women who had no friends and little to do in these "concrete boxes." She said that she tried to get these women to come to her cooking classes when she saw them in the hall. Another older woman who had not worked since her marriage rushed over to apply for work at the new community center across the street—not for money but to escape from her four walls and rooms full of nothing but plants.

Condominium residents had the same problems of group living as did the *danchi* and apartment dwellers (and those who lived in company housing). They, too, worried about piano noises. They had the impression that few of the wives worked, with the exception of professionals such as teachers or pharmacists, and that most were either home or attending classes somewhere during the day. The building superintendants felt the same way. This impression contrasts with the image *danchi* women have of one another—that they are involved in *naishoku* or looking for part-time work if possible.

Many of these observations also apply to women living in their own homes, but there are some differences. Usually there are no problems of noise and shared facilities. Fences around homes preserve some privacy; gardens provide both privacy and a place of busy activity for the older woman who needs her days filled. Women in their own homes felt permanent. If they were young, they worried about maintaining good neighbor relations for the sake of their children; if they were older, they talked about the importance of long-term relations. Permanent residents may develop the sort of relations I found in my husband's home town. Women who spent their years as young wives near one another and had watched one another's children grow up were able as grandmothers to sit over tea and reminisce. In Santama City, several women attending an exercise class at the community center were in their forties with children in middle school. All had lived in the area since their children were in grade school, and all now lived in their own homes. They visited one another frequently and went out together. Visits to their homes showed me that they must have been fairly frequent visitors because they knew where things were kept and adopted casual postures and eating habits. Moreover, their conversations had continuity. They were able to discuss one another's children, the PTA, and other women they had known. Although there were *danchi* in the neighborhood, it was the women who lived in their own homes who visited back and forth.

These homes offer a relaxed atmosphere for talking and perhaps quiet as opposed to the constant "people noises" heard in an apartment. Because each home is separated from the outside world by a fence and has an entrance hall that shields the rest of the home from a visitor, these women feel free to visit back and forth. They can preserve their privacy when they desire and open their homes when they wish. Finally, the women living in their own homes are those most likely to engage in volunteer activity.

The type of housing, then, while not perhaps so important as a woman's age or education or her husband's job, does play a role in shaping her daily life. Ownership of the dwelling is not enough to suggest permanence, though, unless the owned home is an independent house. Communal living produces a set of problems and rules of coexistence that are not necessary in independent homes. On the other hand, the dwelling's size and its general condition (condominiums may be more attractive than *danchi,* for example) also affect whether or not the woman is interested in associating intimately with neighbors or with people in other types of housing.

Provided there is a communal hall, women living in housing complexes have an outlet for teaching their skills or learning new ones. This is more difficult for women in independent homes; if they wish to teach, they must advertise for pupils. The same holds true for the woman who wishes to study something.

Whether or not there were any real differences in income, education, age, or permanence of residence, the women I interviewed in the various housing milieus defined their situations differently. And some of these differences affected their friendship formation patterns and their propensity to participate in civic affairs and other outside activities.

6   Home and Family

Eugene Litwak argues that kinship, friendship, and neighborhood groups continue to have important functions in contemporary society. (See, for example, Litwak and Figueira 1968 and Litwak and Szelenyi 1969.) As primary groups they are best equipped to deal with nonuniform tasks, that is, tasks that are impossible or too costly to be dealt with by experts. Kinship groups are most helpful where long-term contact is needed. Friendship groups, because they are voluntary, may be most useful when neither the nuclear family nor other primary groups have much expertise. Neighborhoods deal with immediate tasks, facilities such as child care, and socializing related to day-to-day activity. The high visibility of coresidents of a neighborhood also helps in friendship formation. The neighborhood may also place burdens and limitations on the housewife, however. Will there be pressure on the housewife to overcommit herself to the organized activities of the neighborhood or to socializing with other housewives? What can she do about it? Above all, what will people think?

The question of the housewife's role must also involve consideration of other family members. The traditional Japanese division of family responsibility was to assign the home and its budget to the housewife and the outside work to the husband. Today, married women comprise a large proportion of the female labor force, and outside activities for women are on the increase. In this context, how do housewives view the question of sex roles?

Recent national surveys indicate that support for the statement "men work outside the home and women take care of the home" ranges from 80 percent (both men and women) to a low of 48.8 percent (women). (See Fujin ni kansuru 1974, 98, and Sōrifu 1978, 174–175.) The reverse question—whether women agree with the statement that it is all right for women to work outside the home and men to take care of the home—has to the best of my knowledge not been asked. I obtained the following survey responses to the first question ("husbands work outside the home and wives take care of the home"):

Agree	49.3%
Neutral	43.9%
Disagree	6.7% (N = 223)

When the opposite question was asked ("wouldn't it be all right for wives to work outside the home and husbands to take care of the home?"), I obtained these responses:

Agree	15.7%
Neutral	47.5%
Disagree	36.8% (N = 223)

Although there is not a great deal of agreement with the second statement, there is a large amount of neutrality. In interviews this doubt was expressed as "I would not want that, but it's all right if someone else does it."

A profile can be drawn of the women who chose the conservative responses (agreement in the first case and disagreement in the second) and those who gave progressive responses. The conservative women tend to be older, they do not work or only do *naishoku,* they say they are too busy at home to work outside, they do not plan to work in the future, and they tend to have less education. In contrast, the more progressive women tend to be in the middle years (thirty-six to forty-five), are employed full time or are unemployed because they have small children or cannot find suitable employment, plan to work part time in the future, and have more education.

The slight difference in outlook varies with age and education, but the responses cannot be clarified without considering how these women may have interpreted the question. Interview respondents tended to reply to probes in this direction as follows:

> Of course women are not inside the home any longer. We go to the PTA and can attend circle activity if we want to.

> In terms of work, yes, this is true, but I am hardly ever at home.

The primary role of the husband *(ikka no shujin)* is almost universally described as being the financial support of the home. His work determines the family's residence, its activity schedule, and the times when the housewife is free to leave the home. In other words, a woman's outside activity is constrained by her husband's work schedule.

In regard to equality between men and women, there is almost universal agreement that men are superior to women but women have tasks to perform that men cannot do, such as child care. The general definition of male superiority is based on the work demands of the salarymen husbands of the majority of the women interviewed. The salaryman's work keeps him away from the home most of the week; he returns home late at night, often after his children are in bed. The housewife accepts this behavior as necessary for his professional success. It is also an indication that men are superior to women—physically because they can take on such commitments and mentally because they can single-mindedly devote themselves to a job. The interviewees made the following comments:

> It's obvious that women are not equal to men. There are no women company presidents, are there? [Thirty-year-old high school graduate]

> Of course, men are superior at everything. The best chefs are men. [Forty-seven-year-old high school graduate and cooking teacher]

> Men and women have different roles. Men are too impatient to deal with children, and women (because of childbearing and their menstrual cycle) can't work as hard as men physically. [Thirty-three-year-old university graduate]

As for the type of husband a woman desires, there is a saying that a good husband is healthy and absent. It is often suggested that Japanese housewives prefer their husbands not to interfere in household affairs because this might lessen their control. Moreover, several interviewees told me that they are only able to participate in so many outside activities because their husbands are absent long hours. I have already noted that when the husband is home, the housewife's outside activity may be cut back. For the woman who is engaging in outside activities merely to fill her empty hours, the husband's absence may be the main reason for her activity. As one interviewee put it: "I don't know why Japanese men marry if they are never going to be home. If my husband were home more, I wouldn't feel the need to go out at all."

The women I surveyed indicated that they want husbands to give priority to their families. In fact, their husbands give priority to work. When asked "which of the following types would you like for your husband?" they responded as follows:

Work priority	40.1%	
Family priority	59.9%	(N = 182)

When asked "which of the following types is closest to your husband?" they gave the following answers:

Work priority	60.0%	
Family priority	40.0%	(N = 195)

Younger women tend to choose family priority and older women work priority. Although the numbers are small, women who are Christian or members of a New Religion prefer family-oriented husbands, whereas members of a traditional Buddhist sect prefer work-oriented husbands. Obviously, these women do not necessarily have what they want. Husbands giving family priority tend to be blue-collar workers or to work in or near Santama City and have family incomes of 4 million yen or less. Those giving work priority tend to be white-collar workers or self-employed and to work in Tokyo. Their family incomes tend to be 4.5 million yen or more. The family-oriented man is either the young husband whose family is still in the expanding stage and whose income is still low or the blue-collar worker who is freed from some of the obligatory after-hours socializing. The work-oriented man is an older salaryman who plans no more children and is probably at the peak of his career or a self-employed man who works at home.

Wives of salarymen often wish that their husbands paid more attention to the family, but few men do so. The wives who prefer the family-oriented husband are similar to those who prefer the less traditional sex roles. They are young, highly educated, and have plans for their own futures. The women who prefer the work-oriented husband are the older wives of salarymen and wives of shopkeepers (or otherwise connected to a family business). Again, these are the groups that have more conservative attitudes toward sex roles.

Two other questions may illuminate the situation. What time do husbands return home, and how do they spend their nonworking days? The husbands of women in the middle-age bracket (thirty-six to forty-five) return the latest (after 9 PM); most husbands of women over

Table 4. Time Husband Returns Home by Respondent's Current Membership in Group

	Time Husband Returns			
Membership	*Before 7 PM*	*7–9 PM*	*After 9 PM*	*Number*
Member	33.3%	35.5%	31.2%	93
Not member	46.2	32.1	21.7	106

forty-five return home before 7 PM. Naturally, men whose place of work is closer to home return earlier. This is also true for self-employed and blue-collar workers. It is the white-collar worker at the peak of his working years who returns the latest. Husbands of women involved in groups tend to return later than husbands of women not so involved. (See Table 4.)

How husbands spend their free time depends somewhat on their age and occupation. Younger husbands, white-collar employees, and self-employed men are more likely to spend their days off with the family. Older men and those in blue-collar positions are slightly more likely to take their leisure without the family. The family orientation of the New Religions is reflected in an extremely high ratio of husbands of believers who spend their free time with their families (76.5 percent in contrast to 50 percent for other religions). In every category, however, most husbands spend the better part of their free time with their families.

Without longitudinal data it is impossible to tell whether the high percentage of young men spending free time with their families is simply a life-course phenomenon or a trend that indicates change. Indeed, it may indicate a modified version of the "new family." Perhaps the "new husband" chooses to spend whatever free time he can with his family rather than in all-male, work-related activities or private pursuits. A casual look around parks, recreation areas, and shopping centers on weekends indicates that this is the case, but it is too early to tell.

As for the wife's contribution to the family, child raising is weighted highly. She bears almost single-handedly the responsibility for raising her children. Unless the child is in school or involved in other activities, the mother is expected to be constantly available and physically present. The question of babysitters is increasingly raised not only in

the press and television programs but also in the newsletters put out by
city governments, by mothers of preschool children who wish to
attend city-sponsored classes or use city-sponsored facilities, and by
the increase in and demand for "baby hotels," controversial places
where babies can be looked after by the hour or the day. Opinions
expressed in city newsletters, by city officials, and by mothers themselves indicate that this controversial proposal is still a matter for
debate. There is opposition to such babysitting in city facilities on the
grounds that child care is the mother's responsibility. Some see
demands for child care during group activity sessions or classes (usually two hours per child a week) as an indication of the selfishness and
weakness of young mothers. Older women say that they got through
this period without such facilities and the young mothers should do so
too. Young mothers argue that they should be exposed to new knowledge and new people so they can improve their mothering skills. If
such a debate is being waged over child care while mothers are studying, it can be imagined how difficult it would be to argue for child care
while mothers are engaged in recreational activities. Again the young
mothers contend that they need opportunities to meet people and that
two hours a week in day care is a good experience for their children
and good preparation for kindergarten.

Arranging for private child care is more difficult in Japan than in
the United States. Women who tried babysitting pools found that the
responsibility of looking after someone else's children was overwhelm-
ing and the pools broke down. There is also great resistance to letting
a stranger into one's home to babysit. I was surprised during my interviews to discover that most women wanted to ask me about babysitting in America; when I explained the system as I know it, I was inevitably asked about letting strangers into one's home. As one women
said, "when these strangers come into your home, where do you put
your important documents and things?" The assumption is that the
babysitter will search through everything to find out family secrets.

Another problem is time. A woman advocating day care at city
facilities said: "Japanese husbands are not ready to come home and
find their wives looking after others' children." All babysitting has to
be done when the husband is out. Indeed, opposition from husbands is
greater than the objections of wives. Women who use the facilities at
city centers said they had got their husband's approval before going
ahead.

In the United States, child care by outsiders is expected. Couples share a social life that does not include children, and the couple who refuses to leave a child with a babysitter is considered odd. In Japan, the mother is expected to look after the children until they no longer need her care (which may mean they have reached college age or married). Rather than employing a babysitter as a matter of course, the Japanese housewife has first to justify why she may abdicate her responsibility, even for a few hours a week.

Demands for child care are, however, increasing. Government-sponsored facilities for children of working mothers are being demanded and built in most neighborhoods. And, as indicated above, demands for child-care rooms in city facilities are growing stronger. In a few years, it is safe to say, most urban women will have used child care of some sort. Indeed, even today women may join a group in order to get their children in child care. Young mothers are growing more determined to give their children group experience before they enter kindergarten. They cannot use government-sponsored day care centers unless they work, so they turn to the city facility as an alternative. Some women take jobs in order to get their children in day care.

It appears that except for emergencies, most of the women I surveyed had never left their children in someone else's care. In contrast to the 68.7 percent who had left their children in an emergency, 26.1 percent had done so while mother worked and 38.9 percent while mother studied. Regardless of the reason for leaving children in another's care, women who have done so tend to be young, highly educated, live in either stem or extended families, and have husbands engaged in other than blue-collar work. In every case, women currently in some sort of group activity are more likely than others to ask someone to look after their children. Women told me that child-care facilities are necessary not only for the mother but also for the development of the child. Older women said they had not used such facilities because they were not available and there were not many activities for housewives in those days. Active older women thought they would use such facilities today if they were younger.

To whom did the women actually entrust the care of their children? Primarily they left them with relatives. In the case of recreational or study activities, they left them with husbands and neighbors; in the case of work (when husbands might not be available and the mothers had some income), they turned to paid sitters or facilities. In emergencies, relatives and neighbors ranked high on the list. (See Table 5.)

Women with higher education tended to choose paid sitters. In the

Table 5. Percentage of Respondents Leaving Children with Various Caretakers

			Type of Caretaker				
Occasion	Husband	Relative	Neighbor	Friend	Paid Sitter	Other	Number
Recreation	21.5%	49.4%	19.0%	3.8%	6.3%	0%	79
Study	18.3	40.2	29.3	2.4	7.3	2.4	82
Work	12.5	43.8	23.0	0	14.6	6.3	48
Emergency	11.0	50.0	29.4	3.7	3.7	2.2	92

case of leisure and study activities, younger husbands were more likely than older ones to have babysat. In all cases, the use of relatives as babysitters was much higher for stem or extended families than nuclear ones. In all cases also, active women had higher rates of using neighbors or paid sitters for child care (even in emergency or work situations) than those not currently active. (See Table 6.)

Interviewees tended to indicate that they did not know anyone to ask to babysit for them. Only by attending a class or group at a city facility did they meet other young mothers with the same child-care problems. These mothers bolster one another and make requests for continued child care at city facilities. Women who had used these facilities when their children were small and women who are currently using these facilities are encouraged to be volunteers, helping the professionals in the nursery.

Other women said they would not feel relaxed about leaving their children with strangers but would do so if the caretaker was either their husband or a relative. Women fortunate enough to live close to a relative (often a sister or in-law) are freer to engage in activities. These data support Litwak's theory of the functions of the extended family and the propinquity of neighbors in urban society. The presence of relatives should continue to be an important variable in the wife's ability to engage in activities outside the home.

The question of neighbors as a source of child care require a bit of modification. The intervening variable seems to be information; propinquity alone is not sufficient. Housewives with small children do not always know about others in the neighborhood who are in their position. PTA attendance is one way of meeting such women, as is taking

Table 6. Child Caretaker by Occasion and Respondent's Current
Membership in Group

Occasion	Husband	Relative	Neighbor	Friend	Paid Sitter	Other	Number
Group member							
Recreation	17.5%	52.5%	22.5%	2.5%	5.0%	0%	40
Study	20.4	34.7	32.6	4.1	6.1	2.0	49
Work	20.8	29.2	29.1	0	8.3	12.5	24
Emergency	5.6	44.4	38.9	5.6	2.8	2.8	72
Not group member							
Recreation	26.7	50.0	16.7	6.7	0	0	30
Study	19.2	53.8	23.1	0	0	3.8	26
Work	5.6	66.7	22.3	0	5.6	0	18
Emergency	17.0	58.5	20.7	1.9	0	1.9	53

one's child back and forth to kindergarten. These activities, however, are begun after the child is at least three years old and do not solve the problem of a mother with an infant. The earliest date at which a young mother can meet others like herself is when she starts taking the child to the park to meet other children. For the women interviewed, the child-care facilities at the city centers not only allow them to take classes but also to meet women like themselves. It may be no accident, then, that women surveyed who are currently active in groups have a higher rate of calling on their friends for babysitting services.

Use of babysitters or facilities is likely to increase, but they will not replace relatives or neighbors because of the costs involved.[1] The housewives I interviewed were very conscious of the need to manage their household budgets with care and were unwilling to spend money on babysitters. Some were even unwilling to spend bus or train fare to attend classes regularly because it would cut into the budget. Although these women do spend money on home and self, babysitters seem to be an unjustifiable expense. For the most part, and especially in the case of women without relatives close by, being a mother of small children means full-time involvement in child care with almost no opportunity to "engage in adult conversation," as one woman put it.

One of the roles often associated with child care in Japan today is the sending of children to various lessons or activities. Lately the media have presented the image of a young child coming home from school not to play but to attend a lesson or go to a prep school before returning home again to eat dinner and study until late at night. What activities do the children of the respondents engage in? In general, participation rates of boys and girls reflect activities considered appropriate to their sex. Boys participate most in sports and girls in arts and crafts. Next in line for both come study-related lessons. Boys participate less in arts and crafts, and there are few boy scouts. Girls have lower participation rates in sports groups, and there were no girl scouts in either sample. Religious activity is low for both sexes.

Active children have mothers between the ages of thirty-six and forty-five (with the exception of children active in religious groups, whose mothers tend to be older). Moreover, the participation rates of children whose mothers have been active in groups are higher than those whose mothers have never been active. This finding supports the concept of peak years in the life course of the housewife. Not only are these years (between thirty-six and forty-five) the peak of the husband's work cycle and the time he is most likely to be absent from the home, but it is also the time when the children are busiest.

Based on interviewee responses, several factors determine the group participation of children. First is the age of the child—preschool to kindergarten children of both sexes are more likely to attend some sort of art or music class, but children of both sexes soon to take examinations for entering high school or college are more likely to be attending study-related classes. Second is family income—in most cases, an annual income of at least 3 million yen is the cutoff for participation in any activity that requires a fee.[2] The third factor is the father's type of work—children whose fathers work in blue-collar jobs are the most likely to encounter opposition if they want to attend activities or classes, especially boys who want to study music or the arts. One mother told me of her kindergarten-age son who wanted to study piano: "His father said this was nothing for boys, and every day he would come home and quietly sit in that room facing the wall with the tears running down his cheeks. I could have stood it if he had cried out loud, but he just sat there day after day with tears running down his face." (This case was settled by diverting the child's interest to drawing lessons, which were more acceptable to the father.) The fourth factor is the interest of the child—mothers told me that more often than not their school-age children wanted to attend various classes because all their friends were going. Since there was no one for them to play with when they came home, mothers said it was better to go to classes than sit and watch television alone. The fifth factor is the mother's desire to build her children's physical strength by encouraging sports activities.

Mothers described most activities for small children (until they prepare for high school exams) as enjoyable; even studying English tended to be done in groups using games and seemed like play to the children. Mothers feel relieved to know that there are places children can play or be with their friends and regret the lack of open space, the danger of traffic if children play together in the streets, and the problems of bothering the neighbors and lack of space if children get together at home.

Several of the highly educated mothers I interviewed said they were attempting to limit television viewing in their homes and therefore encouraged children to involve themselves in other activities. Women with less education or from blue-collar families did not worry about television and said they watched a lot of it themselves. These women said their children can watch the cartoons from 5 to 7 PM every day; they did not seem to worry about the influence of this much television on their children.

It became obvious very early in interviewing that there are a vast number of organized activities open to children from quite an early age, and joining one group often leads to another. One excellent example is the Children's Theater Group founded in 1972 by a group of mothers who wanted their kindergarten children to see theatrical productions, operas, and the like at group rates. This organization has expanded to include about 10 percent of the population of Santama City.[3] Mothers find out about it by word of mouth or through leaflets distributed at kindergartens and elementary schools. They often go on to join the home library movement. Although the women who are active in these groups tend to have higher education and to be fairly young (in their mid-thirties with children in school), women who send their children to the theater or reading sessions but do not take an active role themselves do not necessarily come from a certain educational level or economic situation.

There are also city-sponsored children's groups based on region of residence. These groups meet infrequently, holding, for example, a summer fireworks evening or butterfly hunt, responsibility for which is rotated among the mothers. These groups appeal more to mothers of elementary school children. Other groups are private and may range from a teacher coming to someone's home to private lessons in a teacher's home or a larger facility. Children often ask for such lessons because their friends are attending them. Sometimes, too, their mothers push them, although it cannot be said that all mothers who send children are "education mothers" pushing their offspring to attain as many diplomas and skills as possible. There is in some cases, however, a great deal of standardization, and mothers of children taking piano lessons all proudly told me exactly what page of what book their children were playing at the moment.

In sum, the mother of small children has many responsibilities. Not only must she supervise the children's play and education and consider how best to bring them up at home, she must also weigh the merits of the various activities constantly being brought to her notice through advertising, word of mouth, and the demands of the children themselves. When she moves out of this stage of her life course, this demand decreases. Particularly for the educated mother, however, this stage of life may mean intense involvement in equipping her child with the skills she deems necessary for success. *Q. "stage" is determined by what?*

Entrance examinations for kindergarten place great pressure on mothers of young children. They sometimes indicated that drawing lessons help their small children learn how to print their names and that origami lessons are also good preparation for kindergarten. Above all, mothers want their preschool children to have some sort of group experience before kindergarten so they will learn how to associate with other children and function without mother.

In other words, the various classes and groups for children serve the socialization and skill-building functions that were once handled by letting children play out of doors with neighborhood boys and girls. The glaring fault in all of this was pointed out by one (highly educated) woman who wanted children to have an opportunity to get together on a neighborhood basis: "The children always get together in school classes and are only interested in their classmates when they do get together in the neighborhood. When we were small we followed the bigger children around and learned from them and took care of the little children in our turn. They only know children their own age now." Several of the women I interviewed keenly felt this lack of role models and the opportunity to take care of children younger than oneself, but no one offered solutions.

In addition to almost total responsibility for child care, the Japanese housewife is completely responsible for housekeeping. Contrary to societies in which children are expected to do chores around the house, Japan is a children's paradise in which it is enough for children to study. Older people told me that things were very different when they were growing up and raising their own children. There was no chance then for older children to escape responsibilities, whether shoveling snow, cleaning out the shop, helping with deliveries, or looking after younger children. These days children are spoiled, they said.

Government statistics show that Japanese men spend only a small amount of time on household chores (see Sōrifu 1978, 164, and Fujin ni kansuru 1974, 106–107), and my study too confirms the lack of help from men and boys (Table 7). Daughters tend to give more help to their mothers. The activities in which husbands engage most often are occasional shopping, child care (which includes help with homework), and repairs. Although in every case percentages are very small, it appears that husbands who work in the neighborhood or in Santama City, younger husbands, and those whose wives work tend to help more around the house. This finding reflects comments by interviewees that their husbands were not really unwilling to help; they simply were not around when the work was being done. Men help with shopping, for example, regardless of occupation, probably because it can be done on the way home from work or on the weekend and also because shopping is not defined as unmasculine—in contrast to laundry, which has the lowest rate of male involvement. The interviewees did not expect their husbands to help if they worked in Tokyo or kept salaryman hours. They said it is too much to expect a tired man to come home and work there too.

The shopkeepers' wives I interviewed wished that their husbands

Table 7. Percentage of Husbands, Sons, and Daughters Who Seldom or Never Help Around the House

Task	Husband	Sons	Daughters
Cooking	83.9%	74.3%	45.4%
Shopping	66.5	68.7	44.6
Dishwashing	87.5	87.1	46.9
Laundry	91.5	92.5	75.4
Cleaning	74.6	78.2	54.6
Child care	60.7	86.7	84.3
Repairs	56.3	81.9	97.6

would help. They pointed out that they, too, worked in the shop all day, but when they came home the husbands were watching television and expected them to fix tea or get their drinks. On the days the shops were closed, the men tended to go out together but the wives had to stay home and catch up on the week's cleaning.

The only area in which wives of salarymen wanted more husband participation is child care—not so much for their sakes as for the fathers to get to know the children better. Even then, women were resigned to the realities of the situation. They pointed out that their husbands did not necessarily keep such late hours because they enjoyed it and said that in many cases husbands would prefer to come home earlier. Wives seemed quite sympathetic toward their husbands' lots and said they themselves preferred not to take a full-time job even if they had the opportunity.

In other words, the husband's lot is not seen as an enviable one and the wives do not expect any help. If the husband occasionally does help with a "wifely chore" such as sweeping the walk, the wife is embarassed that he might be seen by the neighbors and she be thought derelict in her duties. Women also pointed out that their husbands had never been trained by their mothers to do anything around the house and had not even been allowed in the kitchen, so what could one expect?

These same women said that they wanted their sons to be self-sufficient so they could help the girls they might someday marry. They did not expect their sons to do chores around the house regularly, but they pointed out that in nuclear families it is very hard when the wife becomes ill or is unable to get things done right after childbirth. They hoped their sons would prove more helpful than their husbands. In the last analysis, however, these women regarded housework as the woman's responsibility.[4] They argued that no woman should take a job if it places a burden (including house help) on her husband and children. One woman put this point very strongly: "If a woman works, she is likely to give 50 percent to home and 50 percent to work. I can't respect a woman like that. If she could give 100 percent to home and still have energy for work, that would be all right. I can't respect a woman who does less than a perfect job at home." (She also said she did not respect women who chose a career rather than marriage.) Every woman interviewed, no matter how busy, indicated that she always managed her home affairs first, so that dinner was always

on the table and (especially) her husband was never put out by her activity. Whether this is true or not is less important than the definition of the sphere of housework as being woman's work. *Why? Seem-a strange cond.*

The women pointed out that kitchens used to be narrow, dark places with little room for anyone besides the cook. Moreover, the cook was usually hidden from other family members. Today, homes are often centered around a dining kitchen, or at least the kitchen is more visible than in the past. Little boys as well as little girls spend their early years watching mother work, not father (unless the father works at home). They become curious about whatever she is doing. They, too, want to try their hands at cooking and cleaning, so the mother teaches them simple things. But no mother was making an effort to see that her son mastered these tasks. Rather, if sons are expected to do anything it is usually to run errands to the neighborhood store, pick up their own bedding in the morning, or occasionally take their plate to the sink or help set the table. Girls, however, are expected to master all the housewifely skills, although interviewees agreed there is little time for them to help. They said it is too hard on children with so many studies and other activities to be expected to help around home as well.

Ultimately, whatever the child's age, responsibility for household tasks rests with the mother. It would seem that with improved appliances and convenience foods, housework could be rationalized and time spent on other activities. Nationwide surveys show that more men than women (73 percent versus 47 percent) agree that this is possible. A slightly higher percentage of full-time housewives (57 percent) than of women in general (51 percent) think such rationalization is impossible. (See *Fujin ni kansuru* 1974, 107.)

Figures indicate that housework time varies. Of those surveyed, 69.3 percent said they spend five hours or less a day on housework, and 67.1 percent said the same for child care (55.3 percent spent three hours or less on child care). Women in the peak years spent the longest time on housework. Women in this period are more likely to have children in elementary school through high school. Women with grown children are most likely to spend three hours or less on housework. Working women also spend less time on housework, especially women who work full-time, have their own businesses, or are in a profession.

In terms of child care, 55.2 percent of those surveyed spent three hours or less a day on child care. Obviously this figure varies greatly with the age of the children. Women aged thirty-five or under spent the most time on their children. Women with small children were the least likely to spend three hours or less on child care (16.9 percent). This figure increases dramatically to 83 percent when children are in elementary school and never drops below that level again.

When children are in elementary school, women are busiest with housework, and housework can expand to fill the hours once taken up by child care. When children get older or leave home, housework decreases and the women potentially have more free hours. This works out well with the life-course pattern already described. The question still remains, however, as to whether housework can be rationalized so that women have more time to engage in other activities.[5]

Based on interview data, the answer is yes and no—yes in the sense that the extremely active women I interviewed had all been active when they had small children. They managed by taking the children with them or placing them in the city babysitting facilities while taking classes. They had managed, as more than one put it, "to become very efficient in doing housework in a short time."

Certain aspects of housework can be dealt with in this way, but others cannot. For example, busy women indicated that they do their housework at night after the children are asleep and before the husband comes home or that they learned to fly around the house in the hour and a half between their family's departure for school and work and their meetings. (Usually everyone is gone by 8:30 AM and meetings begin at 10:00 AM.) Some do laundry at night and hang it out in the morning. Others bake late at night or prepare for their activities then. Mechanical activities can be rationalized and time gained for other activities. These housewives give an emphatic no in some responses. Child care and husband-related activities can be neither rationalized nor delegated. Therefore, housewives are required not only to maintain schedules flexible enough to include attendance at PTA meetings; they are also expected to plan their activities around the return and departure of their families. Rationalization of housewives' activities has not gone so far that women have blocks of time in which to travel distances or work full time without the assistance of a surrogate mother.

In one sense, then, the 57 percent of the housewives in the national survey who responded that housework cannot be rationalized were correct. Insofar as the qualitative aspects of homemaking are the responsibility of the housewife, she does not appear to be able to rationalize this part of her role. There was little indication from my informants that they would care to do so even if they could. Within the parameters of the housewife's role, a variety of life-styles have become possible. To engage in some of these, more rationalization of the mechanical aspects of housewifery is required than in others. (A typology of alternative life-styles is given in Chapter 9.)

Students of Japanese society often point out that the housewife has a great deal of freedom in economic matters pertaining to the home and that husbands are seldom called on to make decisions on the family budget. The image often presented is that of the husband handing over his pay envelope to the wife and receiving back a monthly allowance. According to my interview data, this image is not quite accurate. The income data I received were often vague, but generally a certain sum is set aside each month for the wife to manage. Wives know their husband's salary, but they do not know whether he received any other payments (for extra work or side jobs) or simply do not pay attention to such payments. The wives I interviewed pointed out that a great deal of the monthly salary never reaches home anyway. The company deposits it in the bank, which automatically deducts utility, housing, and credit payments each month. From whatever is left the wife has to manage food and clothing and in some cases put money aside for children's schooling.

The freedom to control household funds is limited, too, by the high price of goods. Women always feel behind in terms of things they need to purchase. They have no allowance for themselves and must judge every yen spent on their own activity in relation to the household budget. Husbands may receive only a small allowance each month, but that is theirs to spend without worrying about other household expenses.

What if the housewife runs short or cannot get to the bank? Is she free to borrow from someone without asking her husband? Of those surveyed, 62.3 percent said they would not consult their husbands if they borrowed less than 5,000 yen. The figure is even greater for women working outside the home (ranging from 72.7 percent for full-time employees to 81.8 percent for professionals). Women in the peak years were also unlikely to consult their husbands (73 percent), and there was a gradual increase as family incomes rose to 5.5 million yen

(56.1 percent with incomes of 2.5 million yen, increasing to 77.8 percent with incomes of 4 to 5.5 million, then falling to 59.5 percent for
over 5.5 million). If a woman wanted to borrow 50,000 yen or more,
86.4 percent would consult their husband. Women in the peak years
showed highest independence (17.2 percent would not consult their
husband versus 4.4 percent for those under thirty-five and 10.9 percent for those over forty-five).

The peak years are also the major years of independent management of one's own home as a housewife. The woman is involved in
most of the formative decisions during that period, and the longer
absence of the husband may require her to make financial decisions by
herself. The limits placed on these independent financial dealings are
within the range of pocket money. Although 5,000 yen is a goodly
sum, it is not so large that it cannot be paid back out of household
expenses without the husband finding out. Fifty thousand yen is
another matter, harder to conceal and more difficult to pay back.
Most women I interviewed indicated that it takes a minimum of
120,000 yen per month to manage a home. (If extraordinary purchases such as expensive clothing or appliances are considered,
150,000 per month is required. Twenty-three of the thirty-nine interviewees who reported monthly expenditures said they spent between
150,000 and 200,000 yen, not including rent.) The sum of 50,000
yen, then, represents from 25 to 40 percent of these women's montly
budget. It is a sum that would be difficult to manage without the husband's knowing and perhaps hard to borrow without consulting him.
Table 8 shows the amount these women spent managing their homes
every month.

Table 8. Amount Housewives Spent Per Month
Managing Their Homes

Amount (10,000 yen)	Percent	Number (N = 39)
12–13	15.4	6
15	20.5	8
17	12.8	5
20	28.2	11
25	15.4	6
30	7.7	3

The freedom to manage household finances is thus very much lim- 🏷
ited by the husband's income and the small amount of money that is
actually "free." Families unable to pay back "salary loans" have been
known to commit family suicide in the face of unpayable debts. The
freedom of the housewife should be judged less in terms of money,
therefore, and more in the light of her greater responsibility to manage
the household, including finances, by herself and her husband's expectation that she will be able to manage with what he can provide. There
is added pressure in the case of a husband who assumes that her inability to provide his favorite food or drink comes from the poor management rather than from high prices.

Traditionally, the Japanese mother could look to her eldest son for
security in her old age. In urban society, however, with little inheri-
tance to offer children unless the parents own a home (or own their
own business) and no guarantee that even a willing son will be able to
live continuously with his parents due to work transfers, this security
is lacking. Interviewees indicated that they intend to live apart from
their children as long as they are together as a couple. What they will
do when they are alone and aged is another problem.

Younger women are more inclined to hope they can live with their
daughters. They pointed out that, after all, it is women who are at
home together all day long, and it is easier to live with one's daughter
than with a stranger (the daughter-in-law). They also said their daughters were very dear, and they hated to think of leaving them. "Daughters are more affectionate than sons, anyway."

Older women interviewed thought they would manage alone if possible, but that when worse came to worst they would turn to a son.
One woman pointed out that she had already promised her two
daughters-in-law various possessions so they would look kindly on her
and not fight over her belongings.

Women who lived in their own homes assumed that one child
would settle with them and then take care of them in their old age. As
one woman put it: "When we buy a home, we always think of the next
generation." A television program on home owning in the United
States pointed out a pattern of older people selling their home and
moving to small homes or retirement homes. The women at the community center asked me how those people could ignore their children.

Of those surveyed, 59.2 percent said they wished to live alone as a
couple and 9.2 percent wanted to live with a daughter's family.

Women with higher education, younger women, and those married to eldest sons were most likely to want to live alone as a couple or with the daughter's family. Older women had higher rates of choosing to live with the eldest son. There was much less agreement about how to live alone when old: 18.9 percent wanted to live with any child and 18.0 percent with a daughter's family. Younger women with more education preferred a daughter's family, whereas older women and those with less education preferred living with the eldest son or any child. Women married to eldest sons were slightly less likely to choose living with eldest sons than those married to other sons. The former also had a higher rate of choice of daughter's family than the latter.

Thus, the stereotype of expecting a son to look after an older parent does not necessarily reflect present reality. The problem of interpretation of these responses, however, may remain with us until the younger cohort grows older. It is one thing to say in your thirties that you want to live with a daughter's family but quite another matter when you are older and actually have a married daughter. So much depends on the daughter's husband and whether or not his parents need care. Moreover, a great deal depends on what the parent can provide. The daughter's husband might not have resources beyond his salary, and the daughter might be dependent on that salary. In such a case, precedent might make it easier for the aged parent to turn to a son rather than a daughter. Some of the older women I interviewed said they felt closer to their daughters but their daughters had married out of the family and could not now be asked to look after them.

No one foresees a happy solution. With little to offer the next generation, women indicated they could not expect their children to look after them. They hoped that at least one child would be willing and able to do so. From their point of view, it would be nice if the child were a daughter so they would not face the problems of living with a daughter-in-law. Those interviewed were not at all sure that circumstances would allow living with a daughter.

Senior citizens at the community center pointed out other problems of living with children in one's old age. If a young couple purchases a new home, even with the older couple's money, it is essentially the younger couple's home and the older woman is not in control. Without the community center, these senior citizens felt they would never be able to meet their friends because they do not have any private space in their own homes. They also indicated they could not ask their daughter-in-law to pay for entertaining guests, nor could they fill the house with old people. When I visited my in-laws in Hokkaido, however, I observed older people gathering and drinking tea all day long. They were mostly shopkeeping families, so there was an openness about the homes or at least about the main room that allowed for this visiting. Moreover, some of the cakes and tea came from the shop and were not seen as special purchases. There was more space, too, so that people often had their own rooms or sections of the living quarters.

This is not to say there is no trouble between the generations—there is plenty. But in terms of being able to associate with other senior citizens who have shared one's past experiences, the urban area presents more difficulties physically than the countryside. All these factors will someday have to be considered by the younger women who today express the hope of living with their daughters. If these women want to live with their daughters, they will have to raise their sons to live with their wife's mother.

One final point is related to the question of older couples living alone. While I was interviewing, public television was showing a serial drama *(Fufu)* on the plight of just such a couple. Now that the children were all gone, they had nothing in common, it seemed, nothing to say to one another. This serial was the subject of much comment, letters to the editor in newspapers, and special write-ins. My interviewees too were eager to discuss this program. Most indicated they were watching the show and wondered whether the same thing would happen to them when they grew old. Women whose husbands were beginning to disengage from heavy work schedules pointed out that for the first time in years husbands were going shopping with them, and they had taken up joint hobbies.

The problem is one that the current generation of thirty to fifty-year-olds will have to face. For the better part of their peak years the couple moves in two different worlds. Suddenly the husband has to enter the wife's world. With no common friends, friends they have socialized with as a couple, to share the blow of retirement, the Japanese man may at a very early age enter a world of complete isolation among strangers. The women I interviewed saw the problem of reorientation to their husbands as a real issue and wished they had some hobbies in common. Still the question remains: How will the younger women surveyed actually meet the crises of their old age?

I have outlined the housewife's various areas of domestic responsibility, and I have suggested that her outside activities are sharply limited by the demands of homemaking and the family budget. Does the housewife feel like a captive in her home? Does she want to get out? And if so, what does she do about it? Less than a quarter of the women surveyed felt shut in (23.7 percent). Women who had previously been active in groups, those who intended to work in the future, those not in the peak years, those with at least a junior college education, and those married to eldest sons felt shut in more often than others.

When women feel shut in, most put up with it. Others elect to tell someone. Women who intend to work full time in the future are least likely to put up with this feeling and more likely to tell someone or go out with a friend. Women with only a compulsory education and older women are most likely to put up with the situation.

The feeling of being shut in comes at two periods during the housewife's life course.[6] The first is when women must deal with small children in confined quarters with little relief. Interviewees told me that after their second or third child they began to feel child-care tasks were repetitious and wanted to talk to other mothers or just breathe the outside air. They did not want to take jobs or leave their children for a long time, but they did need to get out a few hours a week and talk to adults.

When children are in school, mothers have an outlet through the PTA. They also have some free time to engage in circle activity if they wish, so the feeling of being shut in is not so strong. In fact, interviewees claimed that they did get out. Most, however, said that when they were caring for infants they felt very shut in indeed. Women in *danchi* and company housing also indicated that they wished to avoid being too visible to their neighbors. One woman who was not interested in joining groups said she spent most of her time inside her apartment because she did not want to be involved in any trouble. She said she had a number of good friends she had met when her children were in school, and they often talked on the phone. Most of her friends did not care to join groups or go out much.

The second period during which the housewife feels shut in is when her children are grown (at least in college) and she no longer expects to spend much time on their care or education. This period may also be accompanied by a change of residence. The woman who has lived in a series of company houses may now have her own home, as may the former *danchi* or apartment dweller. If there is such a move during this period, the shut-in feeling is more likely to occur. If she is lucky enough to live in a neighborhood where she has resided since her children went to school and where her PTA friends live—or, even better, if she lives near old school friends or relatives—this feeling of isolation is not likely to arise.

The problem for the isolated older woman may be more difficult than for the younger woman. Older women may have had less experience going out on their own initiative, or it may have been years since they tried. They may feel hesitant about going to a city-sponsored activity alone. As indicated earlier, older women in condominiums feel surrounded by the young and have little opportunity to meet others of their own generation. These women feel cut off and indicate a desire to have a place in society. They feel their usefulness to society is gone, through no fault of their own, and they blame society.

The question of being shut in, then, depends on the stage in life for most full-time housewives. During their peak years it is less likely to be a problem.

7 Contacts Outside the Home

In Japan, the occupation of housewife is often characterized as three meals and an afternoon nap. How does the housewife spend her spare time? For the most part she is near her home or alone. Most of the housewives I surveyed spent less than five hours a week visiting or being visited by friends, and even less time going out with friends or neighbors. The great majority did not take lessons of any kind; of the sixty-eight housewives who did, 56 percent spent three hours or less per week on these lessons.

Use of Spare Time

One of the major factors limiting the housewife's outside activity is the difficulty of fitting her domestic roles into convenient time slots. Other limitations are financial considerations and distances to be traveled. Going beyond bicycling distance means using money not only for the activity itself but also for transportation. It also means using a block of several hours. If one's friends live on the far side of Tokyo, for example, one may only be able to meet them a couple of times a year. Even meeting in Shinjuku, the nearest urban center, would require about four hours (one hour each way commuting and two hours or so for tea and a chat). The housewives I interviewed indicated that for the most part they prefer to use the telephone.

Apart from time and distance, there is the question of justification —not only for spending family funds but for spending time on "frivolity" or hobbies. Housekeeping includes a number of activities that can expand to fill the time available. Cooking, sewing, and cleaning out cupboards can easily fill the odd hours and convince the housewife that she *needs* all that time to manage her home.

A commonly held image is that the housewife spends much of her day watching television. The time spent watching television is difficult to evaluate. Only one woman interviewed said that she really spent her days alone watching television. The other women who watched television indicated that they leave it on while they work. Whereas this habit cuts down on their efficiency and means that they have less time on their hands, they are not just sitting in front of the television. For most of the women I interviewed, television serves two functions during the day. In the morning it is used as a clock so that husbands and children will not be late for work and school; at lunchtime it is a companion for the woman having her solitary lunch at home. The most popular program is a noontime interview show in which a dynamic hostess meets various personalities.

The housewife's spare time does not fall into large blocks; rather, it is sporadic throughout the day and varies with the life course. With the exception of older women who have moved into a neighborhood where they know no one, spare time may be punctuated with greeting one's neighbors and brief chats outside one's home. Moreover, although women who are not looking after small children or an aged person find nothing wrong with engaging in a limited amount of hobby or study activity if family finances permit, they cannot justify spending too many days a week outside the home. The same holds true for going out with friends.

Finally, this very limitation on outside activity is directly related to the housewife's professional pride. In other words, the limitations reflect her place in the family, and her reluctance to spend household money on herself is correlated with her role as manager of the finances. One might compare the housewife's position to that of a priest whose official duties may indeed not occupy the better part of every day. If he were to fill all the odd hours with hobbies or visiting friends, however, he would be subject to criticism. Being available when needed is part of the profession in both cases, as is not spending too much time on oneself.

Women who do engage in a great number of outside activities tend to justify it in terms of their housewife role. They also fit these activities to the limitations of time, distance, and money and insist that the activities be flexible. Usually they justify such activities by saying they make women better housewives and mothers. Rarely do they say it is up to the woman herself to decide how to use the time she has left after completing her housework. Within these parameters, then, to whom does the housewife relate and how?

Friends

Five housewives were sitting around the coffee table in a sunny living room. All were mothers of children in junior high school, all lived within walking or bicycling distance of one another, all knew each other through PTA activities over the years, and all were members of an exercise class at a local community center. We had lingered over lunch and tea for some four and a half hours and they were still in no hurry to leave. Discussion had ranged over topics related to children's education and gossip about various PTA members, and now the subject was sales at downtown department stores. All were interested in going to a sale on fur coats, even though no one intended to buy one. They also were interested in getting out more and trying the food at various restaurants, but not unless they had company. ("It's no fun to go if you have to make the trip and come back alone.") Plans were made in a hurry, and two days later they all set off for a day at a department store.

Relatives, neighbors, friends—all play roles in the life of the urban Japanese housewife, and certain patterns of interaction and functional specialization can be discerned in regard to these categories of relationships. Tables 9 and 10 indicate there is a major difference between the types of persons housewives tend to see and speak to in person versus the types they are likely to telephone or write. These contacts were monitored over a two-week-period. The people in closest physical proximity, neighbors and shopkeepers, are naturally more likely to be contacted face to face.

Percentage of communication does not always indicate friendship, however. The term "friend" may cover a wide range of relationships, from a person one chats with over tea to a confidant in a personal crisis. Here the term includes a variety of persons the housewife turns to for different functions. In this sense, a relative could be a friend if he or she serves the specified function.

Table 11 indicates the percentage of housewives surveyed who have friends in various categories. Housewives tend to engage in relationships that may be carried out close to the home, such as visiting friends and talking on the telephone. Again time, distance, and money limit

Table 9. People Contacted in Person

Relation	Percent
Neighbors	25
Friends made through child	22
Shop personnel	17
People involved in common activities	18
Relatives	8
Friends	5
Workmates	4

Source: "Anke-to no matome" (1979, 33).

Table 10. People Telephoned or Written

Relation	Percent
Neighbors	4
Friends made through child	12
Shop personnel	5
People involved in common activities	25
Relatives	31
Friends	21
Workmates	2
Other	10

Source: "Anke-to no matome" (1979, 33).

Table 11. Percentage of Housewives Having Friends in Various Categories
($N = 227$)

	Friends to Visit With	Friends to Shop With	Friends to Go Out With	Friends to Telephone (do not often meet)
Percentage of housewives surveyed	82.4%	51.5%	35.2%	81.5%

Table 12. Percentage of Housewives Having
Friends in Various Categories by Whether
Housewife Is Currently Active in a Group

Type of Friend	Active in Group	Not Active in Group
Visit	89.5%	78.0%
Shop with	62.1	44.5
Go out with	49.5	24.5
Telephone	88.4	74.5

Note: N = 205 except for "visit," in which case N = 204.

the way the housewife spends her free time. The life course affects the various categories. Fewer women under the age of thirty-six (20.4 percent) indicate they have friends to go out with, but these women are most likely to visit back and forth with friends (84.9 percent). Women in the peak years indicate higher percentage of telephoning (86.2 percent) and shopping (60.0 percent) and going out with friends (49.2 percent). Young wives with little children appear to stay closest to home in terms of friends.

Another factor that makes a difference in friendship patterns is group membership. (See Table 12.) A higher percentage of women currently active in a group indicate friends in all categories than do women not currently active. This finding suggests that once women make friends through a group, they engage in other activities together. Another interpretation might be that women involved in group activity are more gregarious and less likely to stay home in any case, so that with or without the group they might have made appropriate friends.

What sorts of people become the housewives' companions for the various activities? Table 13 indicates that different persons fill different functions for the housewife. Neighbors and mothers of children's friends are more likely to be companions for activities carried out in the vicinity of one's home; school friends and workplace friends play a greater role in telephone conversations and are chosen more often as close friends.

Women currently engaged in group activity consistently show higher than average rates of choice of circle friends and child's friends' mothers for the various activities. This may be due to the opportunity that interest-oriented activites offer for making friends with like interests. If one is not so engaged, it might be more difficult to get beyond a

Table 13. Choice of Associates for Various Purposes ($N = 228$)

Category	Visit With	Shop With	Go Out With	Telephone	Closest Friend
Person in same apartment, complex company housing	5.7%	3.9%	1.3%	—	4.4%
Neighbor	26.3	14.9	7.0	—	16.2
Own relative	5.3	7.0	3.1	20.2	22.4
Husband's relative	3.5	1.8	1.8	1.8	5.7
Workplace friends	6.6	3.9	3.5	9.2	8.8
School friends	6.6	5.3	6.1	30.7	16.2
Circle friends	5.3	3.1	4.4	3.9	4.4
Child's friend's mother	17.1	10.1	5.7	7.9	14.5
DK/NA	6.6	2.2	2.6	7.9	7.0
No such	17.1	47.8	64.5	18.4	0.4

Note: In each question the respondents were asked to choose one category only—those people with whom they most frequently engaged in the activity. Visiting back and forth was prefaced with the term "usually" and precluded occasional visits to distant friends; telephone friends were limited to persons one did not usually see; closest friend required a single selection.

superficial relationship with mothers of one's children's friends. Of course, circle friendships might be maintained even if the woman is no longer active in the group, but having an opportunity to see these friends at group gatherings more than likely reinforces the friendship.

In terms of relationships with one's own relatives, interviewees told me that if female relatives live in close proximity they tend to visit back and forth to the exclusion, in some cases, of friendships with other neighbors. These women indicated that nearby sisters or cousins are their best friends to whom they turn for advice and assistance. Survey responses indicate a slight increase in selection of wife's relatives as closest friends with age of respondent (ranging from 19.4 percent for those thirty-five and under to 29.0 percent for those over forty-five). In the future, contacts with other women through longer years of schooling, work experience, and mutual interests may become closer than those with relatives. The choice of closest female relative varies with residential proximity, as women interviewed indicated they would turn to an older sister, cousin, or aunt if that person lived closer than other relatives or good friends.

In terms of neighbor relations, all the women I interviewed agreed they were primarily involved in "greet if we meet" relationships. Getting together over tea is not popular among neighbors as neighbors, but it may be common among women who live near but not next to one another and who meet through children or groups. Rather, interviewees indicated that they prefer to stand and talk outside. This tendency is quite noticeable and was usually commented on by non-Japanese visitors to my home.

A number of factors may make this type of relationship the Japanese equivalent of the American coffee klatch. In the first place, every Japanese home has its foyer *(genkan)* where shoes are removed. Therefore, one may not really consider oneself *in* the home until one has removed one's shoes and "gone up" into the house. Inteviewees made a distinction between the people they would talk to outside and those they would go so far as to invite across the *genkan*. Moreover, until quite recently there has not been the equivalent of the American dining kitchen where wives can sit and talk over a cup of coffee. Rather, kitchens were small and cramped, like the rest of the rooms, making a casual visit a bit more difficult.

Then there is the problem of visibility. American mothers of young children might sit over coffee while their children play together in the yard or house. Most urban Japanese homes have no kitchen window from which to watch the playing children, nor do the residents of private homes meet their neighbors casually over the back fence while hanging out the wash. High walls tend to preserve the privacy of the residents. Women in urban Japan, like the men, tend to meet in public spaces—on the street watching children at play, for instance, or in the halls of an apartment complex. To move from public to private space requires more of an effort than in a society where it is considered rude not to invite your friend in.

Also of relevance here is the widespread desire to treat everyone equally. Women in *danchi* and company housing pointed out that they cannot make special friends in the housing complex without alienating other women. After all, if one stands on the corner day after day with six neighborhood housewives, it becomes difficult to invite one or two without inviting everyone. Even if one wanted to invite all six, there would probably not be enough room. Finally, as indicated earlier, keeping people out of one's cramped housing helps to maintain a little privacy. With so little room, so much of one's life already common knowledge (husband's place of work, age, salary, rent), and so little space to conceal what one does or does not have, women prefer meeting on neutral ground to preserve one another's dignity.

Despite the preference interviewees indicated for carrying on neighborhood relations in public space, it is clear from Table 13 that neighbors are the people with whom housewives visit back and forth most frequently. In specific terms, older women, those with lower family incomes, those with less education, and those who have lived in their present residence longer have higher rates of visiting back and forth with neighbors. In contrast, women in the peak period are likely to choose mothers of their children's friends; women with higher educations choose school friends; and women currently active in groups select friends made in groups and either school friends or mothers of children's friends.

Interviewees explained that when they were young they did not get to know their neighbors right away. Building up such relations (to the point of visiting one another's homes) either took time or depended on having small children who played together. Older women looking back on their lives indicated that when they were first married they tended to get together with either work friends or school friends if they lived close enough. Then there was a period during which mothers of their children's friends became their most frequent contacts but not necessarily their closest friends. When their children stopped playing with neighborhood children, these friendships waned and the older woman either turned to contacts made through long residence in the neighborhood or made use of increased free time to renew friendships made at school.

The question of economic resources is very important. Women living in their own homes and with no apparent major financial worries told me they try to get together with school friends or work friends or go out together. Women with low family incomes said they could only visit back and forth with neighbors, and then only with neighbors in similar financial situations. They pointed out that if they invite their neighbors in they can manage with only a cup of tea and some inexpensive crackers. They also did not need to dress up or spend money on transportation. For these women, neighborhood contacts are a much more important source of friends than they are for women with more economic resources.

Neighbors are also the persons with whom one goes shopping in department stores. Housewives find these excursions much more plea-

surable when they have company on the train to and fro. Furthermore, they indicated that if the purpose is to shop or window shop it is
best to go with women one sees regularly so that time will not be spent
chatting in a coffee shop. If they shop with neighbors, it is easier to get
together later and discuss the merits of the items looked at before they
make up their minds about purchases.

If trips to films or exhibitions are considered, the preference for
neighbors as companions depends on the respondent's age. Women
over forty-five had the greatest tendency to choose neighbors (26.7
percent), whereas younger women seemed to select companions in
other categories. Again, women between the ages of thirty-six and
forty-five had the greatest tendency to choose the mothers of children's
friends (28.1 percent), and older and younger women chose school
friends more frequently than women in the middle age group (23.3
percent for those over forty-five; 15.8 percent for thirty-five and
under; and 12.5 percent for those between thirty-six and forty-five).

Housewives explained that their choice of neighbors or others was
related to the goal and the planning involved. A trip to a department
store may be organized on the spur of the moment; in this case, neighbors are most readily available. (For women in the peak years,
mothers of children's friends might be more readily available.) When
the goal is related to the home or personal shopping, again neighbors
are the preferred companions. When the activity is related to matters
of individual taste (such as attending a film or trying a certain restaurant) and it involves planning (purchasing tickets, arranging household affairs), other friends are more likely to be chosen as companions. The exhibit, lunch, or whatever is a good chance to see an old
school or work friend or someone who shares one's interests.

Just as the salaryman may engage in different relations with his
workmates and his old school friends, the housewives I interviewed
indicated that unless there happens to be a special person with whom
they share interests, their neighborhood relations are centered on their
jobs as housewives. Shopping and children's education are the subjects
of conversation; individual interests are seldom brought out. When
the housewife wants to relate to someone as an individual, she turns to
old friends who knew her before she married.

A new source of friendships is available to housewives today: group
or circle activity. Only time will tell whether these friendships are
maintained. Women who join these activities may become close

friends with others having similar interests. Friends made through circle activities are characterized as women who can be respected (for their skill or dedication) and as women with whom no reserve is needed. Active housewives indicated that they were delighted to meet others like themselves, and it encouraged them to carry on with whatever activities they chose. Furthermore, circle friends tend to live closer than school friends, and increased contact strengthens the friendship. Sharing a common task also brings women in volunteer or civic activities together. Contacts with these friends are related to the activity in which they were engaged. Leaving the neighborhood to attend a play or exhibit is usually an excursion coupled with meeting friends unavailable in the neighborhood. It will be interesting to see what happens to circle friendships in the future. Will these same women choose circle companions over old schoolmates as their closest friends when they are older?

Women also find friends with common interests when their child is in kindergarten. Mothers take their children and pick them up daily, which gives them a chance to see the other mothers once or twice a day. (Some mothers alternate with nearby mothers so that one takes the children and the other picks them up.) Younger housewives indicated that these contacts allow them to be selective (in contrast to neighborhood contacts, where all must be treated equally), and women with common interests who meet through their children's kindergarten sometimes form circles of their own to continue the relationship after the children go on to primary school. Since mothers do not usually take children to primary school, their opportunities to meet other mothers become limited.

School friends are very important as long-term, close relationships. They are the persons most likely to be telephoned along with wife's relatives and are second as choices for going out and for close friends. Women with high school educations tended, however, to choose workplace friends as companions for going out more than did women with higher education, who tended to choose school friends.

This finding suggests that it is the friends one sees regularly during the years between high school graduation and marriage who become closest. If, however, after marriage women are separated from these friends for many years, they may replace them with circle friends or with friends made through religious activities. I interviewed few women who engaged in religious activities, but those who did so indicated that religious group friends were far closer than any other. When housewives form close relations through circles, religion, or other activities they still may choose old school friends as companions when they go out. Such jaunts seem to decline in frequency when they are busy with activities, however, and the relationship to school friends changes to catching up on one another's activities rather than looking for a source of unreserved companionship and advice.

The use of the telephone is also very important for housewives as a means of keeping up with old friends and distant relatives and as a way of relieving loneliness when husbands stay away until late at night. (See Salamon 1975.) Interviewees said they usually call distant friends and relatives when their husbands are out late and the children are asleep. They also said that husbands do not approve of their making or receiving calls (even on PTA business) when they are home. When housewives called me and unexpectedly found my husband at home, they would apologize and offer to call back when he was out, even if the conversation was only to set up a meeting.

Different sorts of friends, then, fulfill different functions for the housewife. In comparison to the opportunities she had at school or at work, the housewife finds her choice of potential friends fairly limited. Furthermore, when such friends are mutually visible (that is, neighbors), she is constrained to treat all equally if they are of similar age. There are two ways the housewife may expand her circle of acquaintances in order to find friends with common interests. The first is by using mothers met at kindergarten or perhaps at PTA as information sources regarding women with similar interests or skills. The second pattern is to join as established group, especially when child care is provided. In this case, women join the group to give the child experience in group situations before kindergarten, to get away from the child for a couple of hours a week, or simply to make friends. Some sort of personal preference enters into selecting the group, of course, but interviewees indicated that more often than not they were less concerned with content than social benefits.

Sources of Assistance

In the course of her duties as housewife, a woman may encounter situations she is ill equipped to handle alone. A family member may become ill, for example, or she may need some information related to child care. Suzanne Vogel (1978, 22) points out that in such cases the woman usually turns to other women, and Linda Perry (1976, 127ff.) indicates the importance of relatives on the wife's side as sources of assistance. It is easy to see why female relatives might be favorite sources of assistance. In the first place, since the housewife is seeking help with a domestic problem, the source of expert knowledge would be other housewives. Secondly, it may be easier to ask one's own relatives than those of one's spouse.

When the task does not require a great deal of effort or involve an invasion of privacy, people met daily in the neighborhood or at work may provide assistance.[1] If a woman is short a small sum of money, for example, she may ask a neighbor or workmate rather than a relative to lend her the amount. If she needs a large amount, however, borrowing it from a neighbor might cause talk and cast doubts on the family's financial situation. In such a case, relatives might be preferred. In fact, my survey indicates that the wife's relatives are chosen most frequently regardless of the amount (55.9 percent for less than 5,000 yen and 64.2 percent for over 50,000). This tendency increases with the respondent's education. For small sums, criteria are related to proximity. Women who are currently employed full time give a lower preference to their own relatives than do women who are not employed or working in other jobs, and these full-time employees have the highest rate of choosing workplace friends.

These findings do not apply to large sums, however. Although the wife's relatives are the most frequent choice in any case, younger women and more educated women choose their own relatives more often and banks and other sources less often then do older women and women with less education. This finding may reflect the presence of a parent from whom the younger woman can borrow and the absence of such a parent in the case of the older woman.

Who provides the care when a family member becomes ill and a helping hand is needed? The wife's relatives are chosen most frequently (51.1 percent in the past and 52.2 percent for the future). Husband's relatives lag far behind in second place (15.1 percent in the past and 16.7 percent for the future), with neighbors and hired help following. Age and education affect the choices. In terms of past requests for help, women over forty-five have the lowest incidence of turning to wife's relatives. Women who used hired help tend to be over forty-five and to have higher family incomes and at least a junior college education. In terms of the future, the same categories of women have the highest rates of choosing to hire someone; those with only compulsory education opt to manage by themselves as do those with lower family incomes. The choice of neighbors for help is highest among older women and those with higher family incomes, and the choice of wife's and husband's relatives is highest among younger women.

Older women may no longer have relatives to whom they may turn in the future. Nor is it surprising to find that higher income leads to greater propensity to employ help and lower income to managing by oneself. The high dependence on wife's relatives, however, supports Perry's conclusions that they are the preferred sources of support and that there may be a change in family ties to the husband's relations. Traditionally the bride married into her husband's family and would probably look for assistance there. The stronger preference for one's own relatives shown by younger women may indicate a change of this type. These are the same younger women who indicated they hoped to spend their old age with their daughters, and the greater freedom to turn to one's own relatives when one is living in a nuclear family may permit changes in this direction.

Another area of assistance is directly related to the question of mother/daughter versus mother-in-law/daughter-in-law relations: advice on child care. Traditionally, the children were the "property" of the husband's family and were raised according to that family's customs. As noted earlier, older women complain that their daughters-in-law turn to books and television rather than to them for advice on housekeeping and child care. It would appear from these comments and from survey responses that the mother-in-law's role is small indeed. Whereas 33.3 percent of respondents chose their own mothers, only 6.8 percent chose mothers-in-law. Written materials accounted for 21.5 percent, friends for 17.5 percent, and television only 1.7 percent. Husbands received just 2.3 percent.

With one exception, no great differences according to age, education, or income are apparent. Written materials are the main source of child-care knowledge for women under thirty-five. This is the only case in which another source was chosen more frequently than one's own mother. The high preference for written materials among younger women is not correlated with education, however. This finding may reflect the increased interest in acquiring up-to-date expertise and the fear that grandmother's knowledge is not enough to meet the demands of today. It may also reflect the lack of written materials in the postwar period (and hence the lower percentage of older women who relied on them), as opposed to the plethora of such works today and the increased ability of wives to afford them.

The low dependence on television may be due to a number of factors. In the first place, the older women in the sample might not have had as much access to television as younger women. Secondly, if the question had be constructed for multiple responses, television might have appeared more often. Based on interviews, however, it is more likely that during the busy periods of child care immediate and specific answers are needed. Women pointed out that it is during the becoming-a-housewife stage that they have time to concentrate on either written materials or television programs related to housewifery. When children arrive, mothers are too busy to read regularly or watch anything. They also indicated that it is most efficient to ask someone who has just experienced what they are going through, but if possible they preferred to ask their own mothers. The media, then, may serve as important sources of information, but the information does not always appear when the housewife needs it. Keeping notes on television programs is tiresome, and so is taking the time and finding the space for newspaper clippings. It is more reassuring to ask someone who has dealt with the same problem successfully.

Friends are the source chosen second to mothers. Housewives may call their mothers long distance to ask about some problem in child care, but they will also seek out friends with children the same age to assure themselves that the problem has been experienced by others. Religious groups offer child-care discussions (and moral education) for mothers, and television programs on child care are constantly being shown; the city sponsors classes for expectant mothers; there are seminars on infant care that will send someone to the mother's home if necessary. Moreover, department stores have baby lounges in which experts (nurses or dieticians) are available to talk about child development; local bookstores are filled with books on the subject; and the city offers courses on child psychology.

For the housewife, however, the three most common sources of assistance for the first child are one's mother, experienced mothers, and child-care books. None of the women I interviewed had turned to her mother-in-law, and after the first few months of child care they used friends as their main source of information. This desire to find friends with whom they could consult was given as a reason for joining circles or seeking out such women in the playgrounds.

What if the wife has a problem on which she cannot consult her husband? Relatives are by far the preferred consultants (52.3 percent); following way behind are school friends (12.7 percent). Women with a university education have the highest rates of selecting either professional or school friends. Those not in the peak years have higher rates of selecting school friends, whereas those in the peak years have higher rates of selecting a child's friend's mother.

Relatives, particularly wife's relatives, are thus the chosen sources of various forms of assistance and tend to be chosen as closest friends over the life course of the housewife. Moreover, there is an increasing tendency to consider one's own daughter the source of security in old age. All these findings support Litwak's thesis of the new functions of the family in urban society.

Friends may serve different functions at different stages in the life course. Whereas during the peak years of child raising, the mother of one's child's friends may serve as consultants and certainly sources of child-care information, during one's earlier or later years the friends (work or school) with whom one spent the years between high school graduation and marriage are more important as sources of assistance insofar as the assistance does not require physical proximity. This finding supports the position that even if school friends are not seen frequently throughout the child-rearing years, these friendships may be maintained and revived when time and resources permit. Furthermore, these friends tend to be more intimate than the persons one associates with when children are small.

Whereas persons close at hand may be chosen in emergencies or for daily companionship, considerations of privacy keep these acquaintances at a certain distance, and the desire to treat everyone equally can act as a buffer against forming close attachments with one or two women. These are professional friends, similar to the friends husbands make in their workplace. Personal likes and dislikes may be suppressed in order not to alienate oneself from sources of information. These are not necessarily close personal relationships. Rather, they are essential sources of information that also provide personal contact in what could be an isolated life.

How women deal with their neighbors often depends on their type of residence. Women who live in *danchi* and company housing wish to avoid "trouble" and the possiblity of rumors preceding them to their place of residence. Women who expect to be in their present home when their daughter reaches marriageable age are concerned about what neighbors will say when investigators come to inquire about the daughter's character. This visibility also affects their membership in groups and activities.

In sum, then, a distinction can be made between the friends the housewife makes professionally and those she makes personally. The contacts she maintains outside her family with relatives, neighbors, child-related friends, and school or work friends are related to their function in her life, to her stage in the life course, and to the professional demands on the housewife.

8 Perceptions of Community and Civic Participation

For the housewife, the term "community" carries with it geographical connotations of the wider neighborhood or the suburban city of residence. (See Tables 14 and 15.) Despite Santama City's constant use of the term "community" in its newsletters and its widely distributed plans to build community centers, less than half of those surveyed and few of the housewives interviewed could indicate what their community might be. The exceptions were women who were active in voluntary and regional activities. These women were quick to respond that their community is their area *(chiiki)* or wider neighborhood and that the next level of community is Santama City. Thus they were more likely to choose their area as the community, whereas those who had lived there for a shorter period were more likely to choose groups (such as hobby or study), family, or workplace. One woman indicated she had always felt ties to her birthplace in Shikoku and, since her husband is from the same place, planned to return there someday. Thus she had not been interested in her Tokyo neighborhood. As her children reached school age, however, she began to realize Tokyo was now their home and Shikoku meant nothing to them. Slowly her attitude toward her present neighborhood is changing. Two years after the interview this woman informed me she was busy doing volunteer work for the blind and taking adult education courses.

Another woman expressed similar feelings, saying she wanted her children to have happy memories of the place they are growing up (in this case a *danchi*). For this reason she hoped to start a book lending and reading group (home library) so children could get together. Women who expected to stay in their present home tended to choose the neighborhood area *(chiiki)* more often than women who expected

Table 14. What Is Meant by Community?

Chiiki (area)/neighborhood	21.9%
Group	13.5
Place for cooperation	16.8
Place to get together	18.7
Human ties	16.8
Other	12.3

Note: N = 155.

Table 15. What Is Your Community?

Santama City	22.3%
Chiiki (area)/neighborhood	27.7
Family	13.8
Child-related	4.3
Work	6.4
Religion	6.4
Friends, "circle"	7.4
Other	11.7

Note: N = 94.

to move. (See Table 16.) The latter tended to list child-related, work, or friends and circle when asked to define their own community.

The women I interviewed agreed they did not want to return to the old country type of relations.[1] Whereas life in the city is sometimes cold because people are not as friendly as in the country, the neighborly helpfulness of the countryside is accompanied by a great deal of knowledge about one another. This lack of privacy means that people are obliged to follow traditional behavior—too great a price to pay, many think, for being able to count on neighbors in time of need.[2] The women thought it would be nice if people could help one another when there is real need, but not get too involved otherwise.

When asked to choose the type of neighbor relations they favored, 57.1 percent of the housewives I surveyed said they prefer to be familiar with neighbors and to cooperate to make the neighborhood a decent place to live (positive cooperation). In contrast, 36.6 percent preferred to participate as required in the area or self-governing associations and maintain appropriate relations with people in whose social debt they stand (necessary cooperation). Only 5.4 percent pre-

Table 16. Community Definition by Respondent's Intention to
Remain in Present Residence

Community	Remain in Residence (N = 50)	Not Remain in Residence (N = 42)
Santama City	21.6%	22.0%
Chiiki (area)/neighborhood	31.4	22.0
Family	13.7	14.6
Child-related	2.0	7.3
Work	3.9	9.8
Religion	9.8	2.4
Friends, circle	3.9	12.2
Other	13.7	9.8

ferred not to associate with neighbors but only to greet them on the
street and leave improving the neighborhood up to the government or
self-governing associations (avoid cooperation).

All those who wished to avoid cooperation were living in nuclear
families. Women during the peak years were most likely to choose positive cooperation. Neither length of residence nor intention to stay
made much difference in choosing positive or necessary cooperation,
but those intending to move and those living in their present residence
less than three years were likely to want to avoid cooperation. Finally,
cooperation is related to the housewife's intention to work in the
future. Women who did not intend to work had a greater tendency to
choose positive cooperation (65.0 percent versus 37.5 percent for
those not intending to work), and those intending to work full or part
time had higher rates of choosing necessary cooperation (full time =
50.5 percent; part time = 37.3 percent; not working = 30 percent).

Those who selected positive cooperation tended to expect benefits
from the neighborhood. Women in the peak period were the most
dependent upon their neighbors not only as sources of playmates for
their children but also as sources of information related to housewifery. If the woman did not intend to spend all her time in the neighborhood or could not contribute fully to such relationships (because of
work or other obligations), she preferred less involvement. Finally,
there was less commitment if these relations were not expected to be
permanent.

A majority of those surveyed indicated their community has no problems at present (82 percent; $N = 150$). Of those who did indicate problems, 28 percent related them to garbage disposal, 24 percent related them to children's education, and small percentages defined them as play areas, pollution, and day care. Women who had belonged to groups, whose husbands were white-collar workers, and who had a junior college education or better were more likely to indicate that the community had problems.

Few of the women I interviewed, however, were able to identify community problems. The problems they did distinguish were related to the woman's stage in the life course and her intention to stay in Santama City. Children's facilities, such as libraries and places to play, were indicated most often; next were places for adults to get together. Interviewees pointed out that Japanese women do not want to go in and out of each others' homes "like Americans do"; they want a place where they can get together outside their homes. They want someone (preferably the government) to take the lead in building such places. Women living in *danchi,* company housing, and condominiums agreed that a public room is necessary to prevent housewives from *"noirose"* (a type of hysteria due to being shut in or cut off from society). Women interviewed also indicated that although they wanted public facilities for getting together, they were a luxury. The only ones who use these facilities are those who can afford to. Other women, when they are finished with child care, take jobs and have no time for such facilities. These facilities, then, are seen as useful, particularly for older women, but not necessary. Interviewees suggested that facilities could serve as places to exchange opinions. Then perhaps people who do want to improve their environment could get together. There is much doubt whether this plan would work, however, not only because working women would have no time to use the facilities but also because women just do not want to get involved.

Another problem cited is the lack of day care facilities for nonworking mothers. A number of women active in groups said this is the biggest problem they face. Not only is such day care good for the mothers, they feel, allowing them to get out and refresh themselves, but it also gives children the opportunity to make friends. A woman who tried unsuccessfully to get her child into public day care was told by a government official that her children were very fortunate because their mother could devote her full energies to them. She retorted that, on the contrary, her children were so unfortunate they could not even obtain day care, and that children of working mothers were much better off. Again, most women are not trying to solve this problem themselves; rather, they hope the government will do it for them.

A Closer Look at Community

When we take a closer look at the question of community, a number of persistent themes appear in interview data that characterize the relationship of the urban Japanese housewife to the world outside her own family. Most of the housewives I interviewed pointed out the importance of beginning any kind of extrafamilial involvement on a small scale. As a woman in a *danchi* put it: "You must be on good terms with your coresidents before you move further out." There are difficulties, however, in going beyond surface relationships. In the first place, if women tend to discuss old age, community problems, and so forth, they will be disliked.

Moreover, there is a tendency, when groups do form, for them to center around a strong leader. When the leader resigns, the group falls apart. A woman long active in an attempt to get *danchi* housewives together in consumer activities pointed out that all the burden fell on two or three people; she ultimately had to resign because it was cutting into the time she needed to keep house. Women who do engage in social service are criticized for their involvement or told that since they enjoy it, why should they ask others to help? Women trying to improve their neighborhood find that even when there are opportunities for women to get together and talk about a problem, everyone just sits quietly and then complains later.

The crux of the matter seems to be the division of labor and the wife's responsibility for the household. It is precisely her role as housewife that motivates her to engage in activities outside the home, but home naturally comes first. The attitude that home comes first inhibits commitment by the interested housewife and gives the uninterested housewife good excuse for not involving herself outside the family. In the words of one *danchi* housewife: "Unless something threatens the household, people do not think community is necessary."

One reason given for the low value placed on participation outside the home is that men are not involved. The husbands of many active interviewees consider their involvement to be "women's activity" and not worth the attention of men. These women indicated their husbands would expect them to drop any outside activity if it made them tired rather than help their wives work for a good cause. As an older woman active in a variety of volunteer and church groups said, "Japanese husbands can accept in principle the idea that it is good for women to be involved in community activity, but they still want their homes clean and dinner on the table when they come home."

The active women indicated that husbands' power, or the power of men, is needed if anything is to be done anyway. It is futile in Japan, they told me, for women to try to do anything.[3] A woman who had tried to get more day care centers built spoke of how patronizing the mayor had been when he came to their area, and she indicated that she had wished there were men in her group to answer the mayor back. Unless men are involved in local activities, the women's husbands denigrate the work they are doing, they are not taken seriously by government, and the activities are deprived of the skills and knowledge that men could bring to them. These women saw no hope for male involvement because of their husbands' schedules. Thus they did not expect community activity to get very far.

The other theme that is repeated over and over is "I want to have it done by someone" *(yatte moraitai)*. Usually this theme appears under the guise of "we need a leader, a strong person, then I'll follow. I don't want to lead." Another version is the demand of housewives for government-sponsored day care for their children even when they are not working. They do not want to organize themselves or take turns babysitting; rather, they want the government to take the problem off their hands. These women want to evade responsibility themselves but might be willing to help if someone else takes the lead.

In some cases, there was a repetition of the theme of not wanting to trouble others *(meiwaku o kakenai)*. The family's problems are to be solved by the family, not by asking others to help. The mother is responsible for dealing with small children and should not expect others to relieve her of this chore. One is not supposed to be selfish or to ask others for help with one's own problems.

One woman told me of her struggle to keep a high-rise building from being constructed next door. She lives in a condominium, and when the new building was proposed her condominium had a residents meeting. At first everyone was willing to sign a petition against the new building, but when it was discovered that only her side of the condominium would be affected, others refused to sign. Finally, she was left alone to engage a lawyer to stop the construction. Although other residents had been asked to do no more than sign a petition, they were unwilling to do even that because the problem was not theirs.

Similarly, women who had taken petitions around either asking the government not to raise day care fees or to build more day care centers were frequently told by older women that because their children were grown, it was no longer any concern of theirs and they would not sign. There is little faith in the effectiveness of acting independent of government. If community is to exist, as one woman put it, "the government has to create it." Individuals do not have the strength, time, or other resources to deal with problems beyond the family.

The housewife views the world outside her home in functional terms. Rather than feeling a tie to her neighborhood or to some broad notion of "community spirit," she separates the functions of various spheres and uses them separately for her purposes. I have already mentioned the function of a place where people can get together and express their opinions about pressing problems. The next step, according to my informants, is to turn to the appropriate agency. If the problem is education, there is the PTA; if the problem is day care, there are appropriate sections at the city office. If there is no section at the city office, perhaps the problem can be handled through the *chō-naikai*.

To the women I interviewed, the functions of residential community are primarily social. The community is expendable. Women indicated that community has nothing to do with them. It is nice for others, but they have no time. Men could not participate anyway, so what is the use? Other than for pure recreation, community is defined as places where local people can get together. It is desirable, if time permits, to develop regional ties. This is particularly true for children who only associate with members of their own school classes and seldom play with younger and older children in the area. Young housewives said they were happy to meet others of their age group at activities, but if community centers were available they could meet older and younger women and develop more of a tie to the neighborhood.

As men become dissociated from the residential community and the livelihoods of their families are less dependent upon it, the "community" becomes expendable—a nice idea so long as it is no trouble, but not really necessary. So long as individual families can get by without such wider involvements, they become similar to hobbies—fine if one can manage time for them over and above home duties.

Rather than seeing the need to involve themselves outside the limited circle of their families, most housewives think that unless their own family requires a certain service they do not need such involvements. Because many housewives are unwilling to engage in activities outside the home, these activities lose strength. Rather than depend on such unreliable means to problem solving or neighborhood improvement, and rather than involve oneself in "sticky" relations, it is better to let the government or school deal with the problems. The few women who do try to deal with problems or participate as leaders in regional activity do so after making sure that their families will in no way be inconvenienced.

The community of the urban Japanese man may well be his workplace, but that of the urban woman is not so easy to delineate. It would include region (as long as she is living in that region) and functional groups such as PTA and child-related study groups (as long as she is in that stage of her life course). School and work friends tend to be important parts of her community insofar as she can maintain contact with them; activity friends may replace these others. If her family is threatened by a problem, she may turn to a group devoted to that problem. Just as her profession as housewife is broad and varies with her life course, so does her community.

Indeed, the wife's networks may stretch wider and cover more variety than her husband's. She may have more opportunity to use her talents and form new primary relationships based on personal attributes than he does through his work-centered life. On the one hand, she can have a kind of professional community centered around her housewife role; on the other, she can have a wide variety of personal primary relationships. Her roles of wife and mother can indeed be supported by such institutions as the educational system and by peer pressure in the neighborhood.

It is not surprising that the woman does not have a clear picture of her community or acknowledge that anything outside the family can claim her commitment. The bifurcation of the work world from the residential world has more than bifurcated the community of the urban housewife. It has split that community into separate functional groups (whether the function is improving schools or making friends), and this very separation is almost a contradiction in terms to the in-group orientation the housewife has received.

Whereas it is easy for the Japanese man to identify his in-group with his place of work, the urban Japanese woman finds it difficult to obtain a continuous in-group. As she moves through the life course she can no longer depend on the same group of women to move with her. When we compare the position of grandmothers in small-town Japan to the older women interviewed in Santama City, this difference is obvious. The small-town grandmothers do not need to look for new friends; they do not have any doubt about loyalties outside the family. For several decades these women have helped one another and have seen that keeping up good relations is vital because of the economic and social interdependence of their families. The urban older woman, however, tends either to have moved or to have seen the companions of earlier stages of her life course move. It is difficult to attach any loyalty to a constantly shifting world.

It is not surprising that the changes in the composition of the housewife's network over her life course have made involvements outside the home seem "nice but unnecessary" or "necessary for a time but not forever." At the same time, the nuclear family cannot handle all the functions the housewife requires, and she must turn outside it occasionally. Even if the housewife does not wish to get involved outside her home, certain aspects of her role as housewife require a degree of involvement.

Participation in Various Groups

Until five years ago Y-san was a housewife pressed by the demands of housework and child care all day long. She suffered constantly from backaches and headaches. Then one day a lecture series at the Asahi Culture Center on "Theories of Personality," which she decided on the spur of the moment to enter, began her involvement outside [the home]. From that time she increased the scope of her interest and activity to include a reading group on psychology, cultural anthropology, English, etc. And now she is eager to put the results of what she has learned into practice in [some kind of] work. ["Onna, koko ni ikite" 1979, 2]

The woman described here actually began her involvement outside the home with swimming lessons and the study of history before the Asahi Culture Center opened; at present she is spending from 20,000 to 30,000 yen a month on tuition for various classes at the culture center.[4] In her words: "My two eldest daughters are already working and from a financial point of view there is finally some money for me to use at my own discretion."

Certainly I would not expect to find a large percentage of housewives able to spend so much money on personal activities. Y-san would be classified as a lady of leisure *(yūkan madam)* who takes a variety of classes to fill up her spare hours. One city official familiar with adult education told me that only such ladies of leisure have time to engage in activities at the city facilities.

Classes represent one of the ways a housewife may use the hours she has free when the children are in school. The entrance of children into kindergarten is the starting point for many women's journeys outside the home, and the push to educate children even before kindergarten in drawing, origami, and the like while giving them a prekindergarten group experience brings women out of the home at an increasingly early age. When asked in a national survey how they would like to spend their free time if they had more of it, full-time housewives indicated sewing, knitting, and other handicrafts (15.9 percent); travel and excursions (15.3 percent); education or study related to daily life (15.3 percent); reading (10.1 percent); and music, art, calligraphy, and the like (9.0 percent). (See Fujin ni kansuru 1974, 316.) The absence of civic activities is striking.

It is not necessary for women to travel to the Asahi Culture Center or to spend large amounts of money in order to study or join activities. City facilities offer a variety of free or inexpensive classes and seminars right in the neighborhood. These activities are held for a short period once a week or twice a month at the time (10 AM to 2 PM) the housewife with school-aged children would ordinarily be home alone. She could complete the activity and return home in time to meet children and feed her family. Some activities may overstep these bounds: PTA meetings may sometimes run late, women may be expected to participate occasionally in evening meetings that include men and women, preparation for school or class activities may require the woman to do work at home, or volunteer work may involve her in activities that could inconvenience her family (including receiving telephone calls).

I found that in every case, however, women who want to make use of these opportunities manage their schedules so that they do their "homework" after children are in bed and before husbands come home. The husband's work schedule is the major factor that prevents women from such involvement. If one husband comes home earlier than most other husbands, for example, this cuts down on the woman's time to use the telephone and do preparatory work.

Table 17. Percentage of Respondents Belonging to
Various Groups

Type of Group	Member	Officer
Leisure	27.6%	8.8%
Child-related	12.3	6.6
PTA (active member)	24.1	11.0
Study	8.3	4.4
Community	3.5	2.2
Consumer	7.5	3.1
Social service	3.9	2.2
Political	1.8	0

Note: N = 228 in each type of group.

The housewives I interviewed tended as a whole to be active in some kind of group or activity. This is to be expected from the means by which I located them (through personal introductions). Nevertheless, there are exceptions: Women living in apartments tended not to be active or to be active only in PTA or other required groups; women helping in the family business had no time for outside activities. In terms of the survey respondents, 46.1 percent were currently active in a nonrequired group,[5] and 41.7 percent had been active at some time in the past. Only 32.9 percent indicated they had never been active in such a group. Those currently active tended to be between the ages of thirty-six and forty-five, to be married to white-collar husbands working in Tokyo, and to have family incomes of 3 million yen or more. Women were active in a variety of different groups and activities, including those related to leisure, study, the family or children, the PTA, local social service, and consumer and political activities. (See Table 17.)

Leisure Activities

A larger percentage of housewives belong to groups related to leisure activities than any other type of group. Members tend to be between the ages of thirty-six and forty-five, have a high school education or above, have children in elementary or junior or senior high school, have a family income of 3 million yen or more, be married to university graduates who work in white-collar jobs in Tokyo, live in their own homes, and intend to stay in their present residence. They are involved in the activity because they are interested, and their rate of involvement increases with lateness of husbands' return home from work.

Since participation in these groups is strictly voluntary and the groups encompass a wide variety of interests, members' backgrounds tend to be varied. Women knowledgeable about who participates regularly in community center activities pointed out that it is primarily women who live in their own homes. If a one-time demonstration is to be given, however, an entirely different group shows up—younger women who live in apartments and can come occasionally but not regularly. I noted the same thing. When I attended single-session demonstrations, I mostly encountered new faces, whereas the women who attended regular classes tended to be older and to take several classes.

The appeal of taking classes or joining a recreation group is obvious. Women who worked part-time told me that if it were not for the monetary loss, they would prefer to take classes. Another appeal of these activities is that they can be done when the housewife feels like it. She need not attend when she is busy, and unless she is an officer she has no responsibility to the group. These activities, then, are the easiest to fit into her schedule and are related entirely to her personal tastes or desire to see friends. In most cases there is very little pressure to complete tasks. Rather, the members bring whatever it is they are making to the class and work on it there. It is up to them to do more, if they have the time and desire.

For some women, these classes may eventually lead to an income. Several women said they were taking knitting lessons because they hoped someday either to teach knitting or do piecework for money. Another woman who expected eventually to return to her husband's rural home was studying how to wear a kimono, because giving lessons in the proper wearing of a kimono would give her something to do in the countryside and because her mother-in-law sews kimonos, so it would give them something in common.

Younger women were interested in cooking or knitting; older women were more interested in Japanese poetry, Noh dancing, calligraphy, or a variety of arts and crafts. Sports are popular among young women (*mama-san* volleyball, for instance); exercise classes find favor among middle-aged women. Older women who were currently active in a group told me they had done a number of other things in the past.

As young wives, most had taken cooking and sewing lessons and then in turn had tried whatever was popular. The current rage was making flowers out of bread dough.

In many cases interviewees said their reason for belonging to these groups was not just interest in the activity itself. (See Table 18.) Rather, they joined to make friends and stayed in to keep up contact with friends. Some said they used these groups to give meaning to their lives when childraising is over. All indicated, however, that the major limitation is economic. Women who had time on their hands now that their children were grown indicated they had tried to make such activities their purpose in life but could not afford to engage in very many of them and therefore still had time on their hands. Younger women said they expected to stay in their current activity until they became pregnant again or it was their turn to be PTA officer. Such activities are time fillers for most women—pleasant opportunities to meet friends but requiring little commitment of time or money and even little commitment to mastering a skill. In most cases, women drift in and out of activities rather than pursuing one for a number of years.

Family and Child-Related Groups

A number of groups bring mothers together out of a desire to do something for their children—for example, children are registered (voluntarily) in regional children's groups when they enter first grade. These groups, using city funds, sponsor school vacation activities such as fireworks and "ghost" parties. Mothers are expected to take turns holding offices, which rotate yearly by address. All mothers of grade-school children are called on at least once. If there are preschool children in the family, the mother can defer her turn until the youngest child is in grade school. Working mothers are not exempt. They are expected to find out what occurred at meetings they cannot attend and to take their part in preparations for events.

Another child-related group is exemplified by the Children's Theater and the home library movement. The former is managed by a few paid staff, but most of the work is done by mothers. Its purpose is to provide opportunities for children to see plays, ballets, and the like at group rates. Originally staffed completely by volunteers, the group hired staff and rented an office when the work of arranging for performances, sending out announcements, and collecting dues became too

Table 18. Reason Respondents Joined Various Groups

				Type of Group			
Reason	Leisure	Child-Related	Study	Community	Consumer	Social Service	Political
Get out/make friends	8.2%	12.0%	20.4%	4.8%	0%	0%	0%
Interest in activity	76.5	26.0	72.2	38.1	73.9	19.0	57.1
Asked by someone	4.1	38.0	3.7	57.1	13.0	47.6	42.9
Health	11.2	NA	NA	NA	NA	NA	NA
Other	0	24.0	3.7	0	13.0	33.3	0
Number	98	50	54	21	23	21	7

demanding. The home library movement, though, is all volunteers and consists of weekly meetings to lend books to children and read them stories. These meetings may take place in a member's home or in a public facility where books may be stored.

In both cases, mothers are encouraged to join when their children enter kindergarten, and most of the women I interviewed indicated that they had been members at one time or another. The advantage of having many members is that one's turn to help out comes up less often. With the exception of leaders in the movement, members indicated that although their children might go more or less regularly, they themselves went only when their turn came, once every three or four months.

Membership is related to the housewife's stage in the life course. The 12.3 percent of those surveyed who were currently members tended to be women thirty-five and under with elementary school children and women with university or high school educations married to white-collar Tokyo workers. They gave as their major reason for joining that they were asked by someone. Officers of such groups tended to be older (thirty-six to forty-five) and to have children of junior high school age.

A closer look at women who are involved actively in Children's Theater[6] or home library indicates that women leaders tend to have at least a junior college education and that former teachers are numerous.[7] At the Children's Theater office I was told that this is not volunteer work because volunteer work is for others and Children's Theater does everything itself. Active women, it was said, tend to be mothers of three children. Either the energy required to keep up with three children is transferred into the group, or women with three children are ready by the time their third is two or three years old to get out of the house—and child-related activity is a good opportunity. A number of these leaders had begun their home library involvement by enrolling their children in Children's Theater and then becoming interested in such activities and starting libraries in their own homes. Not only do they need space to do this, but husbands with jobs that keep them away long hours are an asset.

Children's Theater meetings often take place at 10 AM, so women whose husbands leave for work late often throw off their aprons and run out the door as soon as the husband is out of sight. Leaders in these two groups agreed that it is only because they had time at night free from the care and feeding of the husband that they could get their work done. This activity is very time consuming. Leaders tend not only to participate in their own lending and reading sessions every week but also in the monthly regional meetings of leaders and in one or more related classes (such as children's literature) at city facilities. Moreover, to get funds to buy more books they hold bazaars or help with work at city libraries. Although most of these women started out looking for an activity they could do in or near their home, leaders found themselves involved increasingly in further study, dissemination of publicity, and other time-consuming tasks.

Current leaders indicated that former leaders whose children have grown move on to volunteer or consumer activity, and that they themselves expected someday to rechannel their energies. This activity depends on the commitment of a few well-educated women who see no need to work for money. If one woman holds the group together by doing all the work, it falls apart when she leaves. When the family finances begin to suffer, women turn to *naishoku* (piecework at home) or part-time work. This too has affected the membership of at least one home library group.

Some active women are absent from their homes almost every day. When I asked one busy woman why she did not take a paying job at the library, she responded that she did not want the responsibility. If she were paid she would have to go every day, regardless of her family's needs, but as a volunteer she could give just as much of her time as she wanted and quit at will. In terms of their role as housewife, the leaders all agreed that everything at home has to run smoothly in order for them to carry on their activities. As one put it: "One must be a Total Woman [referring to Maribel Morgan's book by that name] before she can be liberated."

A number of women I interviewed indicated they had heard the home library was a bit "pink" (meaning politically radical) and that whereas they let their children borrow books, they were not eager to join. One of the leaders who had been involved in a Communist women's group dropped this membership before starting her library and refused to participate in any more political activities, such as passing around petitions for better child-care facilities. She indicated that she was still very sympathetic to the political group and kept up with it through her friends, but she had to be careful.

To summarize, membership in child-related groups other than PTA is indeed related to the life course, and all mothers feel a certain social pressure to participate, at least by enrolling their children and taking turns helping every three months or so. Such involvement gives children an opportunity for prekindergarten group experience and mothers a chance to get out of the home. When it comes to leadership and regular attendance, however, not only life course but also life-style is important—women must be willing to use the time left over from home affairs and hobbies for educational purposes. This is an increasing trend among highly educated, younger women, and it will be interesting to return to these women in five or ten years to see if they have channeled their interest elsewhere.

PTA

Membership in the PTA is automatic in those schools that have it. It is definitely related to the life course. At some point during each child's school career, a mother is expected to take her turn as a PTA officer. Interviewees for the most part stressed the compulsory nature of PTA participation, and with only one exception they indicated that PTA offices are taken on as a duty—pleasant sometimes but something to finish up so they can go about their other business. The PTA meetings that I attended turned into question and answer sessions, with mothers asking for advice about individual problems with children, and teachers and principals giving "moral education" to mothers.

A teacher who had been involved in PTA since it began and was now directly in charge of PTA activities pointed out that highly educated mothers question the teachers' approaches and from his point of view create friction. He said that when PTA began in the postwar period, most teachers had higher qualifications than mothers and were therefore respected. Now many mothers have been teachers or have even higher academic credentials and do not always support the teachers. For the most part, however, he agreed that women are avid participants only when they are officers and that most members merely come to the meetings. He also indicated that to get women to attend meetings he annually sends a communication around to husbands and speaks to them on fathers' visiting days, thanking them for allowing their wives to participate. Sometimes husbands are not cooperative, though. A PTA meeting with urgent business to decide, for example, might not end until 5:30 PM, leading irate husbands to call him and ask just what he means by keeping a housewife away so late and depriving him and the children of dinner on time.

Most of the housewives I interviewed regarded the PTA as a necessity but were glad if by chance they were spared the burden of participating. The mothers whose children attended a school without a PTA said they were very glad about this and noted that no one was doing anything to reinstitute the PTA. Other mothers pointed out that by working hard when their turn as officer comes, they hope to inspire their children to work hard at school. After all, they said, if their children knew the mothers were meeting their teachers frequently they would probably work harder. Furthermore, having the teachers know you is probably helpful to your children.

PTA, then, is part of the life course. The degree to which one becomes involved may depend on one's individual interests, but eventual participation as an officer is expected and cannot be avoided without cause. Again, this obligation may mean friction between working and nonworking mothers—the nonworking mothers feeling taken advantage of and the working ones feeling pressured to volunteer for activities on their days off. Although in some cases PTA may be the launching pad to future activity that Higuchi (1975) suggests, it is not the only one nor is it necessarily the major one. Opportunities for study and other activity are providing springboards for women who want outside involvement. Most of the active women I interviewed had begun their activity through means other than the PTA. The older women, however, started with the PTA and then branched out.

Study Groups

Study groups primarily attended by women have reached a takeoff stage in the last ten years or so. A look at the newsletter of almost any city facility illustrates the scope of such activity—ranging from, for example, child psychology to introductory economics. They have encountered problems, however. Once again, women who attend these lectures may be categorized as "ladies of leisure." Furthermore, these groups can only meet when the family is not home, and often no one is willing to take responsibility for leadership, as in the family and child-related groups discussed previously.

These groups also have their own difficulties. In some cases the organizer expects the study to lead to community improvement, but apparently this action seldom occurs. Participants in a course on women's problems indicated that for the most part they found the study interesting but had no intention of changing their own lives. Women who studied consumerism did not necessarily join consumer groups. Rather, aside from the benefits of making friends and broadening their outside contacts, most women keep the knowledge to themselves or use what they have learned to purchase items for their families. With the exception of classes in children's literature related to the home library movement, a great deal of this "study" has no effect on the housewife's behavior outside the classroom.

Appropriate lecturers are not easy to find. Either they are university professors unable to relate to the housewife's specific situation or there is little continuity among the various sessions of a series. Other problems arise from the nature of the housewife's role. Since attendance is sporadic due to home affairs and little preparation can be expected, it is difficult to go beyond the surface for the majority of the participants. Lastly, there is the question of continuity. For example, women who began studying child psychology in a city-sponsored class and wanted to continue as an independent group after the class ended had then to find a means to compensate the instructor. Since most women could not afford a substantial contribution, the study group had to stop or turn into a reading circle.

Of those surveyed, 8.3 percent were currently members of study groups. They tended to be between the ages of thirty-six and forty-five, have junior college or higher educations, have children ranging from elementary school to college, and be married to white-collar workers with family incomes of 4.5 million yen or more. The women I interviewed indicated they began participating after reading about study groups in the city newsletter. Most of the women now in their thirties regarded this as an opportunity to get out and make friends as well as engage in stimulating activity while their children were still small. This was especially true when child-care facilities were available. Most women felt that the mothers of young children need to study —not only do they need knowledge to raise their children properly, but they also need to show their children an image of their mother doing something worthwhile and encourage them to respect learning.

In a number of cases the topic of the study group was related to women or housewives and they joined out of curiosity. Only later did these women discover that they would have to give a report during the course of the seminar and they panicked. The very experience of giving a report led some of them on to other things, however. They had to stand up and talk before the group, and this gave them confidence or led them to take courses on reading aloud. Having to put together materials and a summary about a topic helped these women learn not only what library resources were available but also how to operate copying machines and how to write outlines. For some, these study groups have led to a chain of such groups and the desire to continue in the "Citizens University" (an adult education program) every year. Of course, there were others who left after one group or dropped out along the way because they found the work too difficult.

Although it is too early to tell the impact of study groups on the housewife's activities and community participation—whether she will put this new knowledge and skills into practice or not, whether the demand for women's studies will be replaced by something else, and whether this is just a fad like tennis as opposed to bowling—studying may be categorized as an alternative in choosing one's style of living. Women active in these groups are quick to point out that they do not envy their working husbands; they are much more fortunate to be women who can study. Women these days, they say, are obtaining a broader knowledge than men, and they hope to keep on studying. How this knowledge will be reflected in their future lives remains to be seen.

Civic Groups

Civic groups had the second lowest participation rate among those surveyed. These groups do not comprise a certain type of housewife. The small number of survey respondents who joined them cover the age range and tended to have less education. Interview data show that such groups are composed of women who are personally concerned with a specific problem; thus there is no concentration by such variables as education and income. Those who join to increase the number of high schools tend to be young women who believe their children will be in need, for example, and women who work to increase childcare facilities are usually young, as well.

On the other hand, women who participate in the local women's group *(chiiki fujin kai)* tend to be older, long-term residents. Their concerns are more likely to be related to aging and consumer affairs.

As the vice president of one such group indicated, however, these long-term residents are not eager to get involved in consumer activity lest they alienate the local merchants. Furthermore, a number of these long-term resident members are wives of shopowners and not about to boycott other shops.

As for obtaining signatures on petitions, women agreed that it is *danchi* and apartment housewives who are more likely to sign. Women in their own homes can usually refuse over the intercom or simply ignore the doorbell. One woman who had moved from a *danchi* to company housing recounted that in the *danchi* petitions went around and people either signed them or not. After she moved into the company housing, a small boy rode his bicycle through a hedge out onto the road and was hit by a car. Worried that the same thing might happen to her own children, she went to the housing office to ask if a fence could be built and was told she would have to get the signatures of a certain percentage of the residents. When she wrote a petition and took it around, however, she was accused of being "pink." She never tried to do such a thing again and indicated that she felt alienated from others in the housing project.

Consumer Groups

Consumer activities can cover a wide range—from boycotts to joining a food purchasing co-op. Co-ops were very popular among the women I interviewed. They were not necessarily willing to organize such groups themselves, but most were eager to join and benefit from the fresh produce. Since belonging to a food co-op usually means staying home to take orders or going out to pick up produce, working women cannot ordinarily join. Women in company housing and *danchi* find it easier to participate in such groups because larger numbers mean that deliveries can be made to the housing complex and women can pick up their orders at a central point. Women in their own homes indicated that they sometimes ask PTA acquaintances in housing complexes to order for them.

Among the women I surveyed, 7.5 percent were currently members of consumer groups. They tended to be under forty-five years of age and have small or elementary school children. They usually joined out of personal interest. Older women interviewed who were active in consumer activities indicated they had been more or less involved since the postwar period. Concerned with saving what they could, they developed habits of thrift. Later they were concerned about the new generation who turned to convenience products that led to pollution. These women were eager to teach young women to launder with biodegradable soap and to use parts of vegetables that they now throw away.

Such women all faced a common problem, however, in recruiting young women. One indicated that young women are interested not in local *(chiiki)* cooperation but in getting together with their own age group in activities. Another cited the example of a group she had led in a *danchi*. The young women thought it was better to spend their time earning money to buy a house rather than on her group. A middle-aged woman said that the group fell apart because the burden on the leaders was too great. Rather than every member doing her share in a sale of used clothing, for example, leaders had to do all the organizing and managing. Since the leaders tended to be friends of the organizer, they soon found themselves exhausted by the demands and the group dissolved. A young member said the whole affair was pretty much a one-person show and the ideas were not necessarily applicable to her generation. Young women tend to move into consumer activity after starting a study group. They carry on their activities in city facilities and go to a nearby study center to continue.

Such activity does not culminate in boycotts because, as one older woman put it, "Japanese men want dinner on the table." In other words, wives were unwilling to deprive their families of foods they liked even in an attempt to bring down the prices by boycott. This woman, and others like her, felt that consumer as well as other community or volunteer activities will always be weak unless men joined them. They also agreed that a housewife must never participate in anything until she has taken care of her home and family. Therefore, the women's solution is not boycotting but cooperative purchasing.

Social Service

Social service carries with it an image of the woman participating "because she enjoys it" and being in a comfortable financial position. This is not necessarily a good image for the woman to create in her neighborhood, however. It is better to be seen as working hard for one's family rather than having the time and money to put into social service *(boranteia katsudō)*. Social service volunteers all told me they had been criticized for their activity. One was told, for instance, that her work was useful but she should make sure that when she went out to record for the blind her own family was not suffering. Other women seeking contributions for charity bazaars were told: "Why should we cooperate? If you enjoy this sort of thing, *you* do it." Still others said that neighbors showed them advertisements for part-time jobs, suggesting that if they had free time they should use it to increase their family's income.

The 3.9 percent of those surveyed who were currently engaged in social service tended to be between the ages of thirty-six and forty-five and have white-collar husbands. They joined such groups because they were asked. There were no volunteers in the lowest income bracket, and 55.6 percent of those currently volunteering had between 4.5 and 5.5 million yen in annual family income.

Women active in social service, like those active in other pursuits, indicated the importance of not inconveniencing their families. A woman taping books for the blind, for example, recorded them after her family was asleep at night. She also mentioned a volunteer who spent one day each week cooking and freezing so that she could volunteer on other days. The most common criticism volunteers face concerns finances. Who is to pay their transportation to and from meetings? If they run errands for the handicapped or visit the elderly, who pays for the transportation? They point out the need for government assistance so they can donate time without donating money.

One group, taping for the blind, calls itself the Turtle Group (Kame no Kai) to signify that, as housewives, they can only try to progress like the proverbial turtle, one slow step at a time, and hope they will win the race with the rabbit. With almost no social support, however, not even from husbands, these women do not seem to be gaining in the race.

Perhaps more than any other group, social service volunteers feel the need to prove that they are taking good care of their families. Women who are not currently involved in social service may give lip service to it but in fact do not seem very interested in such activities in the future. They indicate vaguely that if they could afford to it would be nice, but they would rather join study, leisure, or other groups. This lack of social support suggests that as women's activities outside the home increase, development will occur in lines other than volunteer social service work. Some interviewees were openly critical of helping the aged, saying that every family should take care of its own or else the government should look after these problems. Other women indicated that volunteer work seems like an extension of housework (such as folding diapers), and they had enough of that at home. They were looking for something different and interesting.

Political Activity

Political involvement is the least popular activity among the women I surveyed. No characteristics could be determined for the small number of participants. A number of factors enter into a housewife's decision to become politically involved, but political interest is essential in the first place and the husband's work and attitude are also important.

Apparently most women prefer an activity without political connotations. A woman involved in progressive political party activity for some twenty years pointed out that young women are reluctant to join their consumer-related activity because of their political connections. She argued that no one could hope to accomplish anything unless they carried their struggle to the political level. The women in her political organization tended to be long-term residents of Santama City who lived in their own homes and had become active after World War II. Young women, she said, did not realize the importance of political activity. Most of the older women are better educated, and former teachers are numerous.

Like their counterparts in social service, study, and leisure activities, these women, despite their progressive political stance, indicated that they had to leave their home in perfect condition before they could engage in political activity. They said that the housewife must first fulfill her duties and then, if her husband is understanding, she may engage in political activity.

The U.S.–Japan Security Treaty has been of primary importance in raising these women's political consciousness. Most older women had been involved in political activity since the first anti–Security Treaty demonstrations, and a young woman indicated that she did not learn about her friends' college educations until they started reminiscing about what they were doing during the 1970 demonstrations. A second factor that leads women into political activity is participation in a citizens' movement. Often it is recognition of the limitations of these movements—lack of political strength, for example—that persuades women they can best accomplish their goals through a political group, perhaps the women's branch of a progressive political party.

For the most part, though, there is great lack of interest in political activity. The prevailing attitude seems to be that people who are dissatisfied with something should solve the problem themselves. Most of the women I interviewed said they did not understand politics; while occasionally they received literature from the various progressive parties, they found it difficult to understand. They preferred to vote for the person, not the party, and said there are good and bad people in every party. Women who had been involved in political activity when they were students indicated that even if they wanted to continue now, their husbands would not approve. In some cases their husbands were civil servants or worked for a company that did not approve of wives getting so involved.

Past membership in political groups reflects the student or occupational status of the wife. As noted, many younger women in one progressive group discovered they were all at least junior college graduates. Others who had been nurses, pharmacists, or teachers said they had joined because all their friends were members. These women tend to quit with marriage, however, or subscribe to newsletters without going to meetings. When married women join, it is because the political group is attacking a problem that concerns them:

> Just after I quit my job because I could not get my second child in public nursery school, a woman came by with literature on the X Party women's section. I read it and discovered they were working on the problem of day care centers. Since that time, I have been going to the meetings.

Political involvement seems to demand a stronger commitment than most housewives are prepared to make. Not only is the housewife called on to help with more than the specific problem at hand, but she may worry that she does not understand the implications of the party as a whole.

Members of the Sōka Gakkai, a Buddhist sect, indicated support for the Komeito Party for ideological reasons. Highly educated women who are politically active said they support the Socialist Party, for example, because they are against the conservative government but are not as radical as the Communists. Women involved in the Communist Party indicated that they had joined to support a certain program or had joined in college, but they were not so much pro-Communist as anti–Liberal Democratic Party.

For the most part, however, political activity is seen as an aspect of the man's world. To join a political cause, many think, would place too much strain on the household. They are not eager for public exposure. If a petition came around that applied to their lives they would sign it, but they would not take the petition around themselves.

Housewives engage in political activity, as they do in civic or consumer groups, insofar as it does not interfere with their housewife role or place any burdens on their family. The husband's approval is crucial, and leaders recognize that if political tasks take too much of the members' time, they will lose the majority of their membership. Women's participation in political activities, then, will increase with threats to their family's security (neighborhood pollution, for example). But unless the housewife joins for strong personal reasons (past college involvement, an urgent problem, or politically active environment), she will continue to use her spare time for other activities.

At different stages in the life course, the housewife is obliged to be involved outside the home—for example, she takes her turn in PTA. If she wants to keep up her personal relations for the sake of maintaining a communication network, she may find it beneficial to keep up contacts outside the home. In every case, the women I interviewed presented themselves first and foremost as housewives (just as their husbands were first and foremost working men) and selected their involvements outside the home accordingly. Whether in political activity or tea ceremony, the housewife defined her involvement as a way to make her a better housewife and would abandon it immediately if there were any possibility of conflict with her housewife role.

Within the parameters of the housewife role, however, there are a variety of possible patterns of life and a variety of motivations impelling the housewife, as housewife, to engage in activities outside her home. The next chapter examines a typology of these life patterns as I found them among the women I interviewed.

9 Alternative Styles of Living: A Typology

I have raised the questions of change versus continuity in the status and roles of the housewife and pointed out that "belongingness" and status propriety are extremely important. Among the changes are increased life span with predictable periods of greater and lesser home responsibilities, difficulties in maintaining continuous friendships over the years, the likelihood that female kin may not be within easy personal reach, and the development of a host of activities for housewives, including paid work. Among the continuities are the housewife's responsibility for home and children, lack of help from husbands, social value placed on the housewife giving sole priority to home and family, stress on the importance of physical presence and mothering, and the housewife's dependence on her husband.

Given these changes and continuities, the question of status propriety arises. What is the housewife supposed to look like? It is not enough merely to look at housewives' activities to answer this question. I cannot say, for example, that two housewives attending an arts and crafts class have the same motivation. One may be there for purely recreational purposes and the other may intend to teach the crafts one day. I turn, then, to interview data to illustrate the variety of role models available to the contemporary housewife. It must be noted that all the interviewees were full-time housewives. Thus there is no category here for the woman who combines career and family.

Home Is Best

MARIKO

Mariko is thirty-five. She lives in her own home and has two children aged eleven and four. Her husband is forty, a university graduate, and a salaryman involved in sales. She has absolutely no intention of working outside the home or getting involved in classes or friendship that might lessen her effectiveness as a perfect housekeeper. She feels that the majority of her time should be spent on the family.

Her feelings about work come from observing her mother, a full-time teacher who, despite her husband's help around the house, never really had a free moment to relax. In particular, she remembers that her mother was in a terrible position when her own children fell ill— she had to choose between her students waiting at school and her own family. For this reason, Mariko did not go to college. Furthermore, her husband does not favor her working outside the home and does nothing to help her with housework.

She was content just to stay around the house until her second child was about two. It was then she began to realize that she was repeating the same things over and over. She also thought about the approaching day when this child, too, would go to school and she would be alone all day. These thoughts led her to look for some way to broaden her horizons without giving more than a few hours a week. She enrolled in a city-sponsored course on the position of women and signed up for a cooking course. She likes the cooking class but finds the women's course interesting to listen to but a bit too radical.

She wishes her husband could be around the house more. If her husband were home more often, she says, she would not have felt the need to get out. She firmly believes in the importance of devoting her full energies to the home, although she is not against men helping out or women working. She thinks one class a week is the most she would like to be out of the home; as her free time increases, she hopes to concentrate on knitting and spend more time preparing meals and the like.

Her primary involvement is with her children. She is not interested in going out with her husband and leaving the children with someone —not because she thinks they would be endangered, but because she feels it would not be interesting to go without them.

RIEKO

Rieko is forty-four and has two children aged seventeen and thirteen. Her husband, a university professor, is forty-nine. She does secretarial work for him at home about two hours a day. Furthermore, his work-related social life often involves her in parties and occasionally in travel abroad. She is living with his mother and cannot invite anyone into the home when she is there. When the mother-in-law goes to visit other children, she invites her parents and her husband's friends.

She claims that home is best. There are things only women can do, she says, and raising children is one of them. (She is a graduate of nursery school teacher training and has work experience.) Women in Japan today, she says, have adopted a funny image of "women's lib" that is not at all related to the way American housewives live. She thinks that Japanese women should retain their traditional virtues and recognize that little children need a mother's care. Although she never went out, when her son was small he always asked if she would be there when he came back from school. This indicates how important it is that a mother be present in the home, she says.

Her only outside involvement is a cooking class twice a month, which she joined with the support of her husband and children. At present, her work for her husband and her desire to spend as much time as possible cooking nutritious meals for her children occupy her time. She appears ready to transfer her maternal activities to her husband's students in the future and to young couples for whom they have acted as "go-betweens" in weddings.

These two women are representative of a type: the woman who does not want any commitment that might interfere with her primary commitment to the home. Such women think even part-time jobs would consume their time and energy for home affairs, and they seek their husband's permission and advice even for hobby activities. They interpret the role of the housewife to mean quite literally that one should be there to look after the household. They see the question in terms of quantity as well as quality. Moreover, they are completely reliant on their husbands for their present and future welfare.

Long-Range Planner

NORIKO

Noriko is twenty-nine and has two children, one in kindergarten and one in grade school. She has been married nine years to a salaryman with a university education. She herself is a high school graduate who went to night school to study typing and accounting. Although she expected to continue working after the birth of her first child by using public child care, she says that she took one look at the baby and decided to quit her job. After he was a year old, she started taking flower arranging lessons and now teaches flower arrangement as well.

When her second child was born she became interested in kimonos and now works for a kimono dealer advising and selling when there is a sale or exhibition. When she does this she either leaves her children with her husband or pays a neighbor to watch them.

She studies at one of the city-sponsored classes for women and does volunteer babysitting in the nursery for mothers taking such classes. She also works part-time as a housekeeper for an American woman who lives nearby. Her long-range plan, however, is to work in either a department store or for a kimono store full-time after her children are older.

Because the kimono business is one in which age and experience spell respect, she chose it as a career. Thus, with her eye on the future, she has begun to take these part-time jobs at various sales.

She feels that while the position of women in Japan is improving, life is still hard for divorced and unwed mothers. When asked about full-time work for women, however, she says that society should provide opportunities for women to engage part time in specialist activity, that is, fields for which they were trained. To take the woman out of the house full time creates too great a burden on her and she will be forced to quit the job. To make use of women's talents, opportunities should be made available for women to engage in permanent part-time work—for example, while children are in school.

Noriko is an example of a number of women who are studying with the hope of going back to work after their children are older. Whether the work is to be full time or part time very much depends on the type of work. All agree that they are not interested in work that might interfere with their domestic obligations or place any burden on their families. Most of these women, unlike Noriko, think it is unlikely that a full-time job could meet these qualifications.

Once again, the women's commitment is undivided. Work is possible if it merely competes with housework for time (Noriko does her housework in the afternoon while watching her children) but not if it competes seriously for her full-time loyalty.

Civic Activist

SUMIKO

Sumiko is fifty-eight. She has two full grown children and has for the past twenty years or so been active in her local women's group *(chiiki fujin kai)*. This work has involved her in committees, consumer activity such as arranging the sale of fresh produce, recycling used clothing and other items, arranging yearly seminars on subjects such as the Japanese social security system, participating in the yearly bus trip for resident women, and an annual year-end program of instruction in New Year's cooking and flower arranging. She has also been involved in fundraising for some of these activities. She admits that this activity—plus PTA and the like when her children were small and involvement in a citywide group of women's representatives—has kept her busy for years. When she is not occupied with these groups, she may be out visiting friends or going places.

Her involvement in the regional *fujin kai* began when she met a member whose husband happened to be in a field similar to her husband's. When they found they had acquaintances in common, they became friends and ultimately Sumiko was involved in the *fujin kai* and later became its vice president.

She is convinced of the importance of her activity outside the home for two reasons. First, she feels it is important to be of service to the community, although the time and energy spent on such service must not conflict with one's duty at home. She never attends meetings in the evening, for example, saying it is not right that her husband should eat alone. If an overnight trip is scheduled by the group, she will not go. She says that she made these conditions quite clear to the group and if they expected her to be involved in evening activity, she would have no alternative but to resign. (She also says that the extent of her activity is not known to her husband; he never asks what she does all day, and so long as the house is running smoothly she sees no need to tell him.) Her second reason for getting involved is that she feels a woman should not have too much free time. Sitting around doing nothing only leads to complaints which make the home unhappy.

RUMIKO

Rumiko is thirty-six years old and married to a forty-year-old university graduate who works in the field of product distribution. She too is a university graduate, and they have three daughters. From the time the children were very small she has maintained a separation between the adult world and theirs. She and her husband were able to go out and leave the children with her husband's parents next door and were able to put the children to bed upstairs and entertain friends on weekend evenings.

At present she is involved in Christian Church activity two days a week. The home library movement occupies one afternoon a week for lending books, one morning a week for studying children's literature, and two mornings a month for citywide meetings. She also takes turns as a volunteer at one of the city social education centers where she looks after children while their mothers attend classes. She is studying once a week to read aloud to children and tell stories.

She is very motivated by her Christian background to do this type of work. Both she and her husband are active in the church. Although he is supportive of her community involvement, she has not told him the extent of her activities outside the house. (He thinks it is only a couple of times a week.) Since he is gone until late every night, she has time to study and do her housework before he comes home. Her children help, but she is primarily responsible and says that one must be a Total Woman in order to achieve women's liberation. (Maribel Morgan's book *Total Woman* has been translated into Japanese.)

These two women exemplify a number of women who actually spend very little time in the home and yet do not go very far from it. They arrange their activities so that they create no burden on their family, and often they do not tell their husbands the extent of their involvement. They make use of their husband's long absence from the home to get housework and study done without inconveniencing him and are not interested in commitments that would conflict with their primary role as housewife. They tend to become very efficient at housework. Often they make special efforts to please their husbands, fixing their favorite foods and so forth, so there is no question of neglect of duties.

Personal Education

Hisako

Hisako is thirty-nine years old and has two children aged twelve and nine. Her husband, aged forty-three, is a blue-collar worker in a factory. Both are high school graduates. She is actively involved in her local community center, has a part-time job at a supermarket, is a PTA officer, and has joined a group studying mathematics. Moreover, her work with the PTA has led her to join a regional group that plans children's vacation activities and undertakes projects such as eliminating vending machines selling pornography.

She is very busy and away from home most of the time. She deals with housework by rising early and getting everything done before 9 AM. Her husband is cooperative, though, in the sense that he does not object if she goes out to meetings when he is home. Since they are seldom able to do things as a family, she has a great deal of freedom.

She is quite frank about her wish to be active in all her various involvements. Unlike most women who say they are only taking an office because it is their turn, she is eager for the experience and will continue at the community center as long as they ask her to stay on the committee. She has a primary motivation: her own education. She says that since she is only a high school graduate, she never had a chance to study many things and is eager to learn from her own experiences. Another motivation is the desire to keep up with her children's mathematics so that she can help them. This is why she is studying mathematics.

She points out, however, that a housewife's outside activities are limited by her duties at home. Thus she is not interested in a full-time job or one that would prevent her from going to PTA and the like.

EMIKO

Emiko is fifty-one, college educated, and the mother of two sons, one working and the other studying for college examinations. Her husband, a college graduate who works for a broadcasting company, is fifty-five. She takes classes at the condominium where she lives, table tennis lessons at the local grade school, and studies Noh dancing.

She points out that she would not be interested in work of any kind even though most of her college friends teach or do something part time. She has been very busy with her various classes, going out four times a week, but intends to cut back to three times per week.

She believes that a woman should not work full time because it places too much of a burden on the family. If a woman can do both, though, it is all right to work. In her case, she is deeply involved in crafts because she had no opportunity to do these things before marriage. She was young during the war and is now trying to make up for all the lessons and so forth she missed. She says that most of her friends feel the same way and all want to learn as much as possible.

These two women are representative of the housewives who use their spare time for their own personal betterment. They incur only those obligations they can manage within the framework of housewife and do not allow any conflict or competition between the two roles. They expect no reduction of their duties as housewives and regard their activities as opportunities to make up for things they missed that are ordinarily experienced by women before they marry.

Searcher for Meaning

MASAKO

Masako is forty-seven and has two children, one of whom is away at college. She is a high school graduate. Her husband, a university graduate employed as a government engineer, is fifty-two. She teaches cooking four to six times a month at home, sometimes helps a maker of Japanese confections *(wagashi)* when a spare hand is needed, and studies leather tooling as a hobby. She would like to study more things but says a housewife does not have that much money to spend on lessons.

Over the years she has always studied cooking or done various crafts. For the past several years she has gone to work during the summer and New Year's gift-giving seasons at a department store in the Ginza, but now because of the distance from her home (about a one-hour commute each way) she has given that up and concentrates on teaching cooking.

She has always used her money for herself, often going on trips with friends. She is concerned about the importance of having friends as one gets older and tries to involve older women in her cooking classes. She does not like to stay home and is always looking for ways to get out.

In her experience, young women are content with child raising and concentrating on their families. When they reach her age, however, women have to face the question of their purpose in life *(ikigai)*. She and her friends are annoyed with a society that offers no employment for the older woman. She suggests that working at marriage halls, where she would advise young people on appropriate wedding dress, thank-you gifts, and the like, is a job much more suited to the older, experienced woman than to the young girl. Her friends would all like money for their old age, but there is no way to earn it. So they try to find their purpose in life through hobbies. She herself wants to expand her teaching and says that hobbies alone are not enough.

Nevertheless, she does not believe that women with small children should go out and work. Nor does she believe that the household should be taken care of by anyone other than the housewife. Rather, she argues that when the household no longer requires so much of a woman's time, there should be a way to use her talents in society. This is not in any sense a desire to reevaluate the role of housewife; it is only an attempt to point out an anomaly in the position of the older housewife who is potentially useful to society but cannot find a place in the working world. She also says that men are superior to women in every field and that women have their own work in taking care of children.

Role Models of Tomorrow?

For the full-time housewife, obviously the motivation to be a good housewife as defined by society is predominant. Any activity that might limit achievement along these lines is dropped if at all possible. Yet even with these constraints the contemporary woman has a wide variety of alternatives available to her. These alternatives are represented in the preceding typology. (Another option would be to work full time as a career woman, of course, but such women are not included here.)

The important question here concerns the fifth type: the searcher for meaning. Only time can tell whether or not this is a true type. In the sense that it represents a motive for engaging in activities, it is indeed a type. It is also a socially constructed alternative insofar as Japanese society offers no channel through which older housewives can make a contribution or use their skills.

Women currently in the Home Is Best category may become Searchers for Meaning outside the home. Long-Range Planners may be able to avoid the problem altogether by preparing themselves for work in the future. In theory, many of the study groups and hobbies are expected to fill empty hours after the children are grown. What will happen in practice remains to be seen.

The recognition that this empty period will come is widespread among young housewives. This realization itself encourages them to develop a hobby or skill to fill their time when they are older. But hobbies have their limits, as we have seen, so we may anticipate a growing demand that society use the talents and expertise of these women. New roles for older housewives, then, will be one area for future research.

Another question is whether increased recognition of the "meaning in life" problem will lead to an increase in Long-Range Planners who intend to work outside the home after their children have entered school. Rather than housewives rejecting child care and other responsibilities completely, there is likely to be a greater demand for socially constructed opportunities (work and other pursuits) or new roles for the housewife when she is past the peak years of child care.

At present it seems that any new role will have to fit within the parameters of the woman's primary role as housewife, but an increase in new opportunities should lead to greater social recognition of these alternative life-styles and increased motivation for engaging in such activities. The women constituting these various types today are role models for the future—and we may be certain that new role models will appear in the years to come.

10 Toward a New Kind of Community

Despite the great changes that have taken place in the role set of the Japanese housewife, the primary importance of the family still comes across strongly. This family orientation reflects social structures and values, and husbands are not necessarily encouraged by society to be more free than wives. Each has certain duties. The husband should support his family, work hard and move up the promotion ladder, and not squander his income on amusement or become an alcoholic. The wife in turn should put up with his lack of participation in family social life.

The wife has her duties, and the contemporary husband should not complain if she goes out when these duties are done. The value structure into which Japanese are socialized emphasizes the importance of carrying out one's duties well. Work and responsibility have traditionally been valued in Japan, and in many ways acceptance of the housewife's participation in leisure activities or study groups represents a major social change.

In one sense, the housewife's community is her family. It provides permanence, solidarity, and informal primary relations. Families cannot handle every function, however, so housewives go outside of it for other forms of solidarity and primary relations. Family itself is not enough.

One potential solidarity-producing institution is the PTA, which, as Higuchi Keiko (1975) points out, may give women more leadership training than their husbands. A housewife can exert considerable leadership—in consumer or civic activities, for example—but it is almost always limited by interruptions due to the husband's job and child-care responsibilities. The solidarity provided by the PTA is concentrated in the one or two years a woman serves as an officer. Thus although it may be a stepping stone to other involvements, it is so much a part of one stage in the life course that it cannot serve as a solidarity-producing institution of a continuous nature.

Two other potential solidarity-producing institutions are the neighborhood *(chiiki)* and the "circle."[1] The *chiiki* may lead to solidarity among residents of a common area; the circle may lead to solidarity among women with like interests. Problems of local solidarity have already been mentioned, but the most important is that women *move*. Thus they tend to have more interest in circles, which may be dropped at will, than in local relations beyond ordinary polite greetings. Furthermore, real dependency upon one another is related to the life-course periods during which the mother requires a network of information about her children's education. If the family resides in the area long enough, solidarity becomes important when investigators might inquire in the neighborhood about the family's character before a marriage proposal is made. This lack of interdependence and the fact that children become the source of friendships between mothers cut down on the age-related vertical ties in the region.[2] The circle may be a strong means of friendship formation, but there is little interdependence outside the circle itself. Because of the lack of members' commitment to one another, it cannot be said to be a solidarity-producing institution.

The weaknesses of these three groups may be summarized as follows. The PTA is an institution that reaches most housewives, but only for a short period of time—members come and go, and in-depth involvement tends to be concentrated during a one or two-year period of leadership. The neighborhood, which comes closest to the traditional concept of community, includes by virtue of residence all those within its boundaries. With diminishing interdependence and the presence of short-term residents, however, this solidarity is weakened. From the administrative point of view (government funding), the neighborhood may still be the natural unit of community, but its residents no longer necessarily know one another. Rather than vertical ties and long-term interdependence, neighborhood relations tend to be horizontal—based on children or senior citizen's groups, for example —and only for the duration of one's stay. The circle, which may indeed produce solidarity from the point of view of common interests, is a voluntary activity that reaches only those interested and can make no claims on their loyalty.

I have suggested that another focus of solidarity is housing. In testing my hypotheses I found that, contrary to my expectation, very few company housing situations include the husband's superiors. As people move up the promotion rank, they move out of company housing, thus reducing some of the vertical strain I had predicted. However, the desire to keep up good relations with everyone in the company housing complex is reflected in the interviewee's desire to keep a low profile, to avoid asking other wives for help with babysitting and the like, and to join activities outside the company housing project. Kinoshita Ritsuko (1983) describes a similar pattern for wives in company housing.

Public housing seemed to offer the widest scope for interpersonal relations. Though *danchi* women, like company housing women, wished above all to avoid trouble, they were not as concerned as company housing women with their relations with people living around them. Because their husbands' jobs were not involved, they did not become intimate with close neighbors and did not assume that neighbor opinion could hurt them in the long run. The *danchi,* then, provided more personal freedom in (or less constraint on) choosing involvement both in and outside the housing area.

Based on the rates of participation and the interview data, we can draw some conclusions about housing and community. Rather than type of housing per se, permanence is the deciding factor. If a woman expects to reside permanently at her current address or to associate permanently with her present neighbors (as in the case of a company housing project where people may expect to be in another project together in the future), the weight of her neighbors' opinion increases. Women living in *danchi* who do not expect to move are more concerned about their neighbors than those who expect to be temporary residents.

Another factor related to the question of housing is whether or not the wife has to work to help the family purchase a home. Women in *danchi* and company housing who do not have to work (either because they expect to move in with relatives or because they have given up the idea of a home of their own) have more time than working women to consider engaging in local activity and associating with local women.

Group facilities play an important role in building solidarity in a housing project. If there is a public hall, women tend to identify themselves as residents of the project. Furthermore, there is a greater chance to meet women from different age groups in such a milieu. However, the greater opportunity to meet coresidents does not help to integrate the newly arrived older woman into the "community." Unless these women have a skill to teach or an interest in circle activity, they are likely to be isolated.

Housing does serve as a looking glass on the outside world, however, and women not living in independent homes see themselves as less fortunate than those who do. Moreover, the degree of privacy in the various categories determines how much freedom the women feel they have to associate with other women.

Housing, then, may be an intervening variable, but like the question of circle participation it is not enough to know that a woman lives in a certain type of housing without understanding the circumstances. Some *danchi* residents may be permanent; some women in independent homes may be working to pay off the mortgage; some company housing projects may include vertical rankings and some may not.

In terms of a primary level of identification, housing milieu is useful —for example, "I live in X *danchi*." It is useful in understanding the opportunities for group participation and casual friendship formation available to the woman, as well as the degree of visibility or privacy she may have. Housing is not necessarily a solidarity-producing mechanism, however.

What, then, can we say about urban community for the housewife? Can we accept Ferdinand Toennies' assumption (1957, 231) that relations based on concord, folkways, and mores such as kin, neighborhood, and friendship are being replaced by relations based on legislation and public opinion? If so, has Santama City built a community spirit?

At present Santama City is still a paper community. Housewives still see neighborhood cohesiveness as something the government should manage rather than something that has a claim on their time or requires a commitment from them. In other words, the personal benefit to be obtained from civic involvement has not yet proved itself. Thus the neighborhood as a basis for community is regarded somewhat like circle activity—nice if you have the time to involve yourself outside the family, but not necessary. Of major importance here is the generational desire to escape the "sticky" traditional relations found in the hometowns of respondents. Younger women find that a blasé attitude is useful in protecting their privacy. They need an "external enemy" to bring them together. Since the presence of external enemies is localized and sporadic (construction of a building blocking sunlight, for example), this is not a feasible means of integration for a mobile population. Also, since residents are not necessarily permanent, neighborhood alone will not serve as community.

On the other hand, the residential neighborhood cannot be ignored. There is general agreement that people who share common living situations improve their individual lives by getting along and helping each other. No one I interviewed wanted complete isolation.

The world of the contemporary urban housewife is indeed a floating world: Nothing in it is permanent except her immediate family. With this concept in mind, the discussion of how to build community spirit becomes largely irrelevant. One cannot assume that the family will be permanent residents of an area; nor can one assume that the children will maintain associations formed during childhood.

Residence in a specific location is as often as not perceived to be an accident. One may live there because of a work transfer, because it happens to be convenient for commuting, or because one cannot afford to move. Some people, of course, choose the area deliberately, but they do not seem to be in the majority. The ephemeral nature of the "local community" loosens commitment to the neighborhood, but it may strengthen commitment to its various functions. The housewife residing by chance in an area has to operate within the parameters of that chance location. Without a real hierarchy from which to draw leaders, the woman's achievement tends to be judged by how well she manages her home and children. Although her children's educational attainments give her prestige, they are judged by universal standards whereas the woman's prestige is limited in scope. A woman may have high prestige in her PTA because of the success of her children in school, for example, or because she is a good PTA officer. If she moves outside this sphere, however, this prestige is not generally transferred to other organizations in which she might be a member.

In considering the question of community in contemporary urban Japan, then, the following points are important. First, little attention has been given to the mechanisms of communication and integration among members of a mobile population. Second, insufficient attention has been paid to the benefits of solidarity. If interpersonal relations are no longer seen as permanent or related to the family's financial welfare, the family may be reluctant to invest its time in the area.

Third, even if cooperation among neighbors is recognized as a good means of solving problems such as garbage disposal or consumer matters, there is a lack of leadership and knowledge about available human resources.

More attention should be paid to a society-wide network of functionally related associations in which a mobile population can be quickly integrated. This type of organization is exemplified by the Children's Theater group and by the cooperatives for purchasing foodstuffs. Women who move from one place to another can rejoin these organizations in their new place of residence.

The development of such networks, along with the increase of study opportunities for women, if properly integrated, could lead to a new kind of community with society as its unit. Residential location would be purely accidental. In such a system, the achievements of women could be put to good use and the problem of meaning in life dealt with. Common purpose—rather than common residence—might serve as the basis for solidarity. This solidarity in turn would be based on a realistic recognition of the housewife's life course and the importance of the home. Both community development and community theory have come to a crossroad. If we shake off the traditional notion that a new residential-centered community will develop and instead give more recognition to women's study groups, we may come closer to a realistic approach to solidarity in a mobile society.

I began by asking what a housewife does all day. I have indicated there are a variety of things she may do. A better question is what *will* she do all day? Will opportunities be created for using her skills without unduly depriving her home of her time? Will study groups end there, or will women start to put their study into practice? If the answers to these questions lie with the women themselves, I expect little change. The ephemeral groups will continue, but community spirit will not develop. There is little support for "civic activities."

A small-scale approach will only lead to a continuation of this situation. Women will have little opportunity to form solidarity organizations. If, on the other hand, real benefits accrued to such activity, if volunteer activity were reflected in an improvement of the individual family's circumstances, if social support could be channeled for such activities, and if women's skills could be marketed when they are in the quiet periods of the life course, then new forms of solidarity organizations might grow. The women I interviewed spoke of starting small and working outward. Social education, not only of adults but of children, might stress the benefits to be gained from such solidarity. Government funding for one class for a year might help launch, say, a nationwide network of consumer activities. Women might be encouraged by the presence of child-care facilities to invest their skills in improving society. Changes might occur.

I do not intend to end this study on a note of utopian speculation. Rather, I want to suggest that the current situation is extremely ambivalent. The women I interviewed really do not have a community in the sense of solidarity-producing institutions outside the family. Nor is there any indication that such institutions will grow out of the residential setting. If citizen participation is desired, the formulation must be based on a society-wide transformation. Otherwise, as in Santama City today, "community spirit" will be left to the government and perhaps the long-term residents but will not touch the majority of the population who see themselves as transients.

Appendix:
Methodology

Between the end of November 1976 and the end of January 1977, I was able to spend ten weeks in Tokyo. This period laid the groundwork for my study. Most of the ten-week period, with the exception of the Christmas–New Year's holidays, was spent collecting materials from various sources or consulting with Professor Aoi Kazuo of the Sociology Department, University of Tokyo, about the research site. This work also involved meeting appropriate officials at the Santama City Office and visiting the community center to ensure that it was suitable for participant observation and to obtain the permission of staff and local residents to do observation there. Since all the observation I had previously done was in America, and since I obviously was going to be conspicuous in an all-Japanese group, I wanted to learn what would happen if I were to join a group of Japanese housewives engaged in some craft or other activity.

It so happened that I was living near Santama City at the time and my own city newsletter announced cooking classes for local women. The classes were to be given at the city hall and were to last for four weeks; the subject was to be New Year's Cooking. The class was fully booked when I registered, but one person dropped out so that I was able to join the last three sessions. About twenty-five women were in the class and we were divided into groups of five with each group preparing the entire menu for the day under the teacher's direction. This meant that although I would not have much contact with the other twenty women, I would have close contact with the four women in my group. After the cooking was done we ate our creations and compared the work done in the various groups.

The classes lasted two hours and afterward everyone rushed off to do her shopping and get home to take care of the family. I discovered that after the initial surprise of my teammates at finding themselves stuck with a foreigner, everyone was so busy cooking that little notice was taken of me. The only times I felt conspicuous were when the cooking demanded skills not usually acquired in American kitchens, especially the delicate use of the Japanese cooking knife *(hōchō)*, and my rather unartistic slices caused friendly joking. Once a woman came up behind me to ask a question about my technique. When I turned around she jumped and gasped—she had not expected to see blue eyes!

The cooking class kept us all so busy that the other members of my group and I had little time to talk at all, and we decided to meet for coffee right after New Years. The four other women included one who appeared to be in her early thirties and had two small children (she was the wife of a taxidermist and sold kitchen products on the side) and three older women with children in late junior high or high school. The taxidermist's wife lived behind her family shop, two of the women lived in their own homes, and one lived in a purchased apartment in a *danchi*. They were very interested in my life and although I did not tell them I was doing graduate work I did say I was still studying. I had to return to America for one more semester, I told them, and would be back (to join my husband, I said) in May.

Our discussions were a good chance for me to ask indirectly about such matters as life-styles in various housing categories and to find out what sorts of things these women were involved in. Often the subjects came up without my introducing them. The woman who lived in the *danchi*, for example, talked about the variety of classes she had taken over the years, and the other two who lived in houses replied that she had access to many more activities than they because she lived in a *danchi*. She agreed that her large *danchi* offered opportunities for activity. Since the *danchi* included a large shopping center and a public hall, there were bulletin boards for announcing classes and also a place to hold them. However, she said that in a *danchi* it is impossible to single out people for intimate friendship. Rather one has to keep up the appearance of treating all of one's stairwell mates equally, and this can create an artificial formality and stunt relationships. The other two house-dwellers agreed that they did not have such problems but did not have access to so many classes either. These discussions helped me in formulating questions for my interviews later. We met once more before I returned to America. This second meeting was held at the taxidermist's home and was a waterless cookware party. We were all a bit taken aback because it was obviously a sales promotion and we all thought that we were just going for tea. For my purposes, all this discussion was excellent practice. Not only was I able to accustom myself to the way that Japanese housewives in such situations relate to one another, but I was able to listen to what they talked about among themselves (mostly family matters and the ever-popular subject of classes or going out to eat). After I returned to Japan in May 1977 we met four times (minus the taxidermist's wife who was always too busy to get together). The first time we visited nearby botanical gardens; the second time we had a pot luck lunch at the *danchi* woman's home; the third time the two women living in houses came to my home for lunch (the *danchi* woman had moved to another city); and the fourth time we had lunch in a local restaurant before I left Japan.

I valued this opportunity to slip into a Japanese women's group not exactly as an official observer but with the intention of getting the feel of what it would be like to be an observer. On the one hand, it gave me confidence before I went into the field, especially in regard to the relationship I could establish as an obvious outsider. It taught me how to listen well and later take fieldnotes in Japanese, and it taught me how to ask questions that did not seem strange or too inquisitive. In other words, I learned how to lead the women to subjects other than cooking. On the other hand, this experience also showed me that Japanese women themselves raise some of the issues that interested me: housing differences, friendship formation, classes, and activities. As a result of this experience I could begin my official observation with less trepidation and avoid a number of blunders—especially the urge to question rather than listen quietly until the conversation turned to an appropriate topic.

I returned to Tokyo at the end of May 1977 and spent the month of June househunting and calling on professors and city officials. Although I had originally intended to live in my research site, I settled in a neighboring city fifteen minutes by bicycle from the community center. In terms of commuting to the community center, I was as close as I would have been in Santama City; in terms of the interview stage to come, I had convenient access to any area of Santama City. And, finally, I could have a bit of privacy when I wanted it as well as a chance to look at women's activities in my own city.

I began observing in the community center and continued to do so through October. (I cut back my attendance toward the end as I began in-depth interviews all over Santama City.) The staff at the community center was extremely helpful, and I was able to select groups for participant observation from a huge bulletin board listing activities for the month. Not all activities were suitable for my purposes. I looked into volleyball, a group learning how to decorate old bottles, and a calligraphy class, for example, but none of these was really suitable. Volleyball kept the members fully occupied for the entire two hours and afterward they all rushed home to lunch. The bottle-decorating class also allowed no time for discussion; it was held in the afternoon and then everyone rushed home to prepare dinner; and, furthermore, the members were few in number. The calligraphy class allowed no time for anything other than practicing the characters for the day. Each person would come in, sit down, take out her tools, and then practice the model the teacher put up. They merely greeted and said good-bye to one another with no chance for gossip.

After trying many classes and meetings I settled on three groups: a tea ceremony class, an exercise class, and a class in ribbon-flower making. On the other weekdays I would attend occasional meetings (PTA gatherings, for example, or a bread making class) or sometimes locate myself in the library, restaurant, or community center office just to observe the flow of women, note the demands for various classes, and talk to women every chance I got. All in all, I was either at the center or at some meeting or gathering on most Mondays, Wednesdays, and Thursdays during the four-month period. The center was closed on Tuesdays, there was not much happening on Fridays, and weekend activity tended to be oriented to husbands and children rather than women's group activity.

I used every opportunity to make myself known. I talked to children's groups about family life in America, made myself very visible in the library and restaurant, and spent time almost every day at the office window dispensing equipment such as Ping Pong paddles and games to those who wanted to borrow them. From the beginning my purposes were made clear to everyone. The office staff and community representatives explained that I was interested in women's activities and life-styles and invited women to sit down over coffee or lunch with me and become friends.

I began my official observation with the women's exercise class. An office staff member introduced me to the class leader who said she would check with the members and let me know if I might join. I spent the majority of my Wednesday mornings with this group. They were the source of many fertile discussions over the next four months. We met at ten in the morning and exercised under the direction of a young teacher (graduate of a physical education college) who was paid by the women. Most of the women (usually about twenty came) were in their late thirties to fifties, and the program as fairly rigorous. After exercises we all swept down the gym floor and replaced the Ping Pong tables. Then the women went home for lunch or ate in the center restaurant.

Several times these women invited me and other members to their homes for lunch or coffee, and these gatherings often turned into gossip sessions and discussion from noon until five or so when everyone rushed off to shop, change clothes, and fix dinner. These women were for the most part familiar with one another's homes. Although the frequency of meetings seemed to increase because I was there and I admitted I was interested in seeing people's homes (as they were in asking me about American homes), most of the women knew where one another's homes were and appeared to have been there before. They knew where living rooms were located and could talk about how much a certain plant had grown, new items in the home, and so forth.

Clearly these women had come to know one another over the years through their PTA participation, and school matters and gossip were often their main topics of conversation, along with shopping and classes. All avidly read the sale announcements in newspapers and frequently discussed which sales they had attended. Occasionally they agreed to go shopping together to look at things they did not intend to buy now but "someday," such as diamond rings and fur coats. The women who visited back and forth like this were for the most part mothers of junior high and high school children and lived in their own homes. Although I could not ask for fear of embarrassing someone, they seemed to be junior high or high school graduates and all had working experience. Their husbands' occupations included television cameraman, Bank of Japan staff member, salesman, a local tailor, and, of course, white-collar salarymen.

The second group I attended regularly was the class in ribbon-flower making. About 10 AM some twelve women would gather (most seemed to come late) around low tables in a tatami room at the center.

In this case the teacher, a gregarious woman in her late thirties, just told me to come along with her and introduced me to the group. Again their ages seemed to range from the late thirties on up, although there were two younger women and one who appeared to be close to sixty. Since the two hours or so of class were devoted to copying the sample flower the teacher brought (each woman brought her own wire, ribbon, and scissors), there was a lot of time for conversational exchange.

The women were very familiar and free in their discussions, although it appeared that some of them only saw one another in this class. They would tease one another about going back home for summer vacations only to meet their childhood sweethearts, exchanged light sexual banter about one another's husbands, and, like the women in the exercise class, avoided formal language. As soon as a man entered the room, however, they became more proper toward one another.

These women did not invite me to lunch or to their homes, but I had numerous opportunities to talk to them around the center and also saw a number of them at PTA and other meetings. A leading topic of conversation was the importance of this class as a means of relieving stress. In fact, they even discussed getting together for tea and gossip during the teacher's summer vacation. Although they had to give up this idea because of vacation activities, a couple of the women said anyone was free to stop by their homes for tea because they too felt the need to let off steam once in a while.

The third group I observed regularly was the tea ceremony class. About twenty women were enrolled, but usually only ten or so showed up. This class was taught in the afternoon by a widow in her sixties. She was a member of the senior citizen's group and lived with her daughter and family about ten minutes' walk from the center. She had always lived with this daughter, even when the couple first married. This arrangement had worked well because the daughter and her husband taught at different universities and the mother then babysat for the two children. The tea ceremony class was organized so that the teacher brought the necessary equipment (tea bowls and whisks) and the students brought their own fans, paper, bamboo, and other utensils for eating the sweets. The students also brought the sweets and the tea and gave the teacher an honorarium for her time. During the two-hour class each student would make tea in turn while the rest of us watched. (Two persons served as guests for each ceremony.) Sometimes we practiced other roles—assistant to the person making tea for elaborate ceremonies, for example, and special guest.

Although there were more people in this group who appeared to be in their fifties, there were women in their thirties and some very young women as well. Most appeared to have studied tea ceremony before they married but had forgotten it. Although each woman was at a different level, some practicing the most elementary stage and others more complex ceremonies, none appeared to be particularly proficient or to practice in between sessions. They all took a light attitude toward the classes, correcting one another in a joking manner, laughing at mistakes, and countering laughter at their own mistakes with "wait until you try."

Twice during the summer the lessons were held at the teacher's home. After one of these sessions, one of the students invited me home for a different kind of tea. Two other women were learning *osencha*—the proper making of tea ordinarily served to guests—from the woman who invited us. During the conversation that afternoon, these women pointed out that their neighbors consisted of two types of women: those who were always involved in everything and those who preferred to stay at home and perhaps work on knitting or something and then show the results to their neighbors. They did not feel that many women fell into a middle category. They also observed that some of their neighbors seemed to regard the community center as a place where people went for classes because they could not afford a private teacher. These women denied this image (they were all comfortably well off) but said there was a difference between the center's classes and private lessons. In their opinion, women took private lessons to really learn something or to go one step further and become teachers someday. Classes at the community center were much more informal and did not lead to certificates or licenses. Women joined them for the purpose of making friends or getting out of the house, not for mastering the art or craft itself.

Apart from these regular observations, I was able to look in on other groups and talk to various persons at the community center. The librarian was a good source of information about the uses of the center, the types of women who used it, and the intergenerational differences she had noted. She suggested that attitudes toward babysitting were changing in the sense that younger women often were willing to watch one another's children while they attended classes (not at night but during the day) and that such a practice was unthinkable just ten years ago. She also told me about the home library movement and suggested that I might wish to learn more about it.

Attending the senior citizen meetings gave me a chance to ask about generational changes and the importance of the community center in their lives. Although they mostly met at the center for recreation, they did have a project for recycling aluminum cans to reduce pollution. The women told me that the aged no longer had a role in Japan; their daughters-in-law (about half seemed to live alone and half with children) did not want to learn from their skills and experience. Many of these older women felt that children were being allowed to run wild these days but said the younger generation laughed at them for being old-fashioned. They had heard that Americans are stricter in child-rearing and asked me about American practices. They were also interested in social security and homes for the aged. Several said that since the postwar constitution no longer required the eldest son to care for his parents, they felt like beggars living on charity. They wanted the nation to provide them with sufficient money to live on and indicated that if there were suitable homes for the aged near their children and friends, many would be happy to move there. In other words, they felt tied down by their present arrangements, dependent on children financially but with no real role to play.

Several said that the community center was a real blessing. Not only did it give them a chance to meet other senior citizens with whom they could talk about old times or share hobbies, but it also gave their daughters-in-law a chance to relax. (Things were really different when they were young, they said—at that time they looked forward to the chance to take their children to the doctors as the only opportunity for getting away from the watchful eye of their mothers-in-law.) Furthermore, these people could not entertain their friends at home. Even if grandparents did have a room of their own (many slept with grandchildren), always having elderly people around was a nuisance to daughters-in-law and a bother to grandchildren studying for exams. If only they had more space, they said, they would love to invite friends home, but several admitted that they could not afford to do so. It was not fair, they said, to ask their children to buy refreshments for their friends out of the family budget.

Other observations during this four-month period helped me organize interviews and the survey. I noted, for example, that women's attendance at group meetings is always subject to interruption—vacations in the summer, school activities the rest of the year—so there is very little regular attendance until children are grown. I noted, too, that when plans are made for buying a home, thought is given as to how their children might use it some day. (This was a frequent comment after a television special had appeared showing how American families may move several times over a lifetime and thought is not usually given to passing the house on to children.) When wives' friends came to visit, I observed that they came as individuals or with small children whereas husbands' friends may come to call as families. Finally, attending PTA gatherings at the center gave me a chance to observe many of the women I met in other classes as they interacted. Again I heard them stress the importance of the PTA as an opportunity to learn about other households, something they cannot do if they are isolated in their own home.

PTA meetings were often held with a teacher presiding and various women asking questions and sometimes receiving advice from other women as well. At these meetings I observed that in order to get children to participate in, say, a campfire, all the preparations have to be made by the organizers. If the organizers just made curry and asked each child to bring his own rice, for example, the children's mothers would not send their children. From these PTA gatherings I also heard a comment that was to reappear in interviews: Children living in the same neighborhood do not know one another; rather, they just know children in their own class at school. In other words, there is virtually no association of children of different ages. Some of the women regarded this as a serious problem and wanted to organize more neighborhood activities to give the children a feel of belonging and teach the older children responsibility for the younger ones.

This period of observation, then, served not only as a source of information and an opportunity to meet the same women in a variety of circumstances but also as a sample from which I could decide how to organize my interviews in stage two of the study. Of course, this preliminary stage as well as the interview stage served as the basis for the survey I administered in stage three.

Because of my interest in housing I intended to interview ten housewives in each of the five housing categories outlined in Chapter 5 (*danchi, shataku,* independent house, condominium, and apartment).

Originally I had hoped to interview one hundred women (twenty in each category), but on the advice of Professor Aoi and others at the University of Tokyo I cut this number back. My experience over the year led me to realize the wisdom of this decision—given the time I had to collect data, the fact that I had to depend on the schedules of the individual housewives, and the need for introductions to these women in the first place. (I did try knocking on doors in a condominium at the suggestion of the super, but only two women were willing to be interviewed after a morning of knocking—and of these two, one was "not home" when I came back on the appointed day.) Interviewing one hundred women would have meant postponing the survey and probably would not have led to much more information. In addition to the fifty women, I interviewed seven community leaders (including one man).

The interviews lasted from one and a half hours, the minimum time necessary to cover all the questions, to most of a day; the average interview lasted three or four hours. Usually I answered all the questions the interviewee asked me so that I could then ask her what I wanted. Throughout the interview I tried to identify with the woman —if she talked about the problems of relating to her husband's family, I mentioned that my husband was the eldest son in his family. In all cases I tried to make the woman talk as freely as possible without feeling that she was being interviewed by an "intellectual." Rather, I tried to emphasize our common experiences and stress my interest as a woman, particularly as a foreign woman married to a Japanese eldest son, in the lives of Japanese housewives. This approach appeared to work very well in most cases.

In only three cases did the interviewees seem ill at ease. One was a woman who had expected me to be Japanese-American and for the first thirty minutes was too stunned by my blue eyes to talk of anything else. One was a resident of an apartment who did not want me to tape the interview but later confided that she was divorced and remarried—something that not one of her neighbors knew and she trusted me not to tell. The third woman had appeared eager to be interviewed. When I showed up she had on a very good kimono, sat me on a sofa, and knelt at my feet for the duration. This interview was awkward, to say the least, because I could not get off the sofa without appearing strange—not only was I in Western dress but there really was no more floor space—and she never got off the floor.

The interviews would not have gone as well had I needed an interpreter. Since most of the homes were small, bringing someone with me would have created space problems and introducing a Japanese in the middle would have broken down some intimacy and meant that I was unable to ask certain questions. As a foreigner I could ask about family relations whereas a Japanese interviewer would have had great difficulty. Moreover, using an interpreter means more formality and takes more time for questions and answers to be translated. Not needing help was therefore a great advantage. I was also quite familiar with Japanese etiquette. I never went into a house with my coat on or attempted to put it on before going outdoors. I knew how to bow after being shown in and when to give my name card. I knew that bringing a cake (a standard 500-yen pound cake from one of the best department stores) would place the relationship on a social basis. I knew better than to jump right into discussion but let a few minutes go by for casual talk and for the woman to ask about me. All of these techniques helped. Many of the women told me afterward that they had expected a huge awkward foreigner who could not sit on their tatami. It therefore relaxed them to see someone who not only could sit but who gave them cake and the proper greetings and who fit into Japanese-size clothes.

I tape-recorded almost all the interviews on a small machine that needed no extra microphone and could be placed on the table or floor and forgotten. I used sixty-minute tapes so there would be as little interruption as possible. In two or three cases the tape recorder malfunctioned and I was obliged to take notes; in two cases I was refused permission to tape. Most women, however, readily understood that it would be very difficult for me to take down our conversation rapidly in written Japanese and that tapes were much more accurate than notes. I, of course, assured them that their identities would be absolutely secret and that the tapes would be transcribed by myself and no one would be given the opportunity to listen to them. In comparing the taped and the written interviews I found that the former were much superior in quality. Not only were the respondents able to talk more freely on tape, but I was able to concentrate fully on the questions, watch the respondent's reactions, and observe the home.

I originally asked women to fill out time budgets and send them to me in the stamped and self-addressed envelopes I provided, but I later dropped this idea. The return rate was sometimes low, the forms were not filled out carefully enough to be of value, and I was able to learn how they spend their days in greater detail than a one-day time budget could give me. Instead of a formal interview schedule I had a list of the topics I wanted to cover. I soon became so familiar with these topics that I could almost dispense with the list. For the two sensitive areas of wife's education and family income, I showed a card so they could just say "number 10" or whatever.

In general, my interviews covered the topics of age, housing type, number of rooms, number of coresidents and relation to respondent, husband's age and education and work, how long married, love marriage or arranged marriage, wife's education, work experience, work plans for future, length of residence, past residence, rent, future moving plans, different types of residences in the past, difference in human relations in various housing types, her personal friends and how often they meet, her group activities, relations with family, guests, other couples, neighbor relations, religion, politics, work, social service activities, civic activities, how she spends her days, time spent on child care and housework, children's and husband's activities and help around the house, use of babysitters, attitude toward sex-based division of labor, what she reads, plans for old age, definition of community, community problems, and how they should be handled. Finally, I asked about family and personal income and how much she spends on housekeeping each month. Within a few days after every interview I sent a handwritten thank you note to each respondent.

The process of finding respondents began in September when I attended a seminar on women's issues at the Santama City Social Education Hall. The staff there introduced three women to me: one in her own home, one in a *danchi,* and one in a *shataku.* From these interviews, making use of further personal introductions, I received a total of seven more interviews. The next source of introductions was a children's literature study group at the same facility. This meeting was attended by members of the home library movement. I interviewed four such women and gained three more introductions to women outside the movement (including a flower arrangement teacher, a woman in the Children's Theater, and a former nursery school teacher who lived in a *shataku*). Nine introductions came through the community center. Three more were direct requests from the social education facility. One introduction came from a personal acquaintance, and this person introduced me to two more women. Four interviews were a result of knocking on doors of a condominium with the head of the city community section. (Possible respondents had been suggested by the super.) One of these contacts led to one more and that one to three more (living in different places). Knocking on doors myself led to only one interview; one more was obtained through a friend and three through the super of a different condominium.

To meet civic leaders I either asked the city community section head or located people myself through suggestions and personal introductions or interviewees. Seven introductions of people living in apartments came through distributors of government literature on children's education who went from door to door covering the entire area.

In all cases I explained the type of people I was looking for and asked their help in introducing people. Many were cooperative but I had trouble locating apartment women—most appeared not to be involved in many outside activities or know many of their neighbors. In a few cases the respondent would promise to telephone people about me, but when I phoned I discovered that the people had never heard of me and were naturally suspicious. I did get three interviews this way but received many more refusals. Personal introductions cut down on the range of women one can meet, of course, but I was able to interview all over Santama City and each housing category included several age groups. With only ten women in each housing category it was impossible to get much variety, so I tried to ask about past experiences of older women and tap the broader knowledge of women who were leaders, teachers, and the like.

The seven leaders I interviewed included a male school principal who had long experience with the PTA, two nursery school teachers (one city and one private), one condominium superintendant, one Children's Theater representative, one leader of a group of mothers of handicapped children, and one leader of the women's section of a progressive political party. Some of the women chosen from housing categories also were leaders or active in various areas and thus divulged information about their activity.

The characteristics of the women I interviewed can be categorized as follows: (1) age: eight women under 31; nineteen between 31 and 35; eight between 36 and 40; eight between 41 and 45; two between 46 and 50; two between 51 and 55; one between 56 and 60; two over 60; and six unknown; (2) income: five had annual family incomes below 2.5 million yen; thirteen between 3 and 4 million; ten between

4 and 5 million; six between 5 and 6 million; five above 6 million; and the rest undisclosed; (3) education: five women had completed compulsory education only; nineteen had high school education; and twenty-eight had further education; (4) husband's education: thirty-one husbands had university or higher education; one graduated from a two-year post–high school trade school; five were high school graduates; and seven were graduates of compulsory education only; (5) husband's occupation: eleven husbands were professionals; twenty-four were white-collar employees; five were self-employed; two were retired white-collar employees; and one was superintendant of a condominium.

Apart from the individual data I collected through these interviews, I received comments which were helpful both in designing the survey and in subsequent interviews. Women in volunteer activities suggested it was wrong for a woman to ask her family to make sacrifices if the activity was only volunteer. If the woman became a real professional, however, then perhaps she could ask children to help around the home. Several women also said they would not be interested in becoming professionals (whether in library work or education of the handicapped) because they did not want the responsibility but preferred to put their role as housewife first. The head of the social education facility suggested that it was women who had time to kill *(yūkan madam)* who made use of his facilities; women in *danchi* and apartments were too busy working to engage in social education and other activities.

The interviews spanned the period from September 21, 1977, to March 9, 1978. During this period I was also busy drawing up the interview schedule for the survey. Because of resource limitations, rather than pretesting the entire survey I tried out individual questions unobtrusively in the process of my interviews and on Japanese women friends as well. The survey underwent several drafts under the supervision of instructors in the Sociology Department of Tokyo University, Professor Aoi, and my advisor Professor Herbert Passin. The survey was not a translation but was drawn up in Japanese.

The sample consisted of four hundred housewives (again the number was chosen in accordance with resource limitations) selected from the Santama City Citizen Register from among the population of all currently married women aged twenty-five and above. This sample of four hundred was stratified by the population of each of the thirteen subdistricts of Santama City to be proportional to the population distribution. Actual selection was made by a senior citizen known by the city office to be reliable for such work. This person was instructed to open the books of the registry at random (several books are kept for each district) and select the appropriate number of women. (If one district called for ten women and there were five books, each book was opened at random twice and two names were written down.) Because the registry was in constant use at the city office and permission was needed to use it, it was deemed more efficient for a senior citizen to sit in the office using the books as they became available. Such a person was more likely than I to avoid mistakes in copying the handwritten Japanese and also was able to copy faster.

The interviewers were ten women university students because I wanted women to interview women and wanted them all to be Japanese. The actual interviewing covered the period between March 18 and May 1, 1978. Interviewers sent out printed cards in advance explaining who I was and the purpose of the survey, assuring privacy, and indicating the day the interviewer would call. Each respondent was given a mechanical pencil as a gift for participating; 230 questionnaires were filled out and returned (57.5 percent); of these, 2 later had to be discarded leaving 228 usable questionnaires; 66 respondents were never in (16.5 percent); 71 refused (17.75 percent); and 33 had moved (8.25 percent).

The return rate varied from district to district, ranging from 75.8 percent to a low 30.8 percent. (In this district several houses had been torn down for urban renewal and the addresses no longer existed.) The return rate also depended on the interviewer. It is always difficult to assess whether interviewers did in fact call back at least three times as requested, but certainly paying only for questionnaires completed was an added incentive. To improve return rates in the future, interviewers must be paid more and perhaps a longer time should be allotted for collecting data. College students, however, are more willing to do such work during spring vacation; not only do many college students go home for the summer but there would be difficulty locating respondents (especially women who take their children home to the country for several weeks).

I am not sure the return rate would have improved if my card had mentioned that the survey had city approval. Although several women refused to respond because it was not a city survey (primarily older respondents), some people told the interviewers they were not interested in cooperating if it was a city survey because there were too many already and they feared information on income and so forth would be used against them at tax time. After talking to experienced researchers before I designed the card, I decided to avoid any implication that this was a city survey.

Notes

Chapter 1

1. Although a variety of housing projects (especially high-rise apartments or sprawling projects) fall under the general term *danchi,* I am concerned here with public housing. This housing may be under the auspices of the nation or the metropolis, but in either case it has certain characteristics. First, available dwellings are allocated by lottery to eligible applicants; second, there are income and family requirements for eligibility. In the case of the *danchi* built under the auspices of the national Japan Housing Corporation (Nihon Jūtaku Kōdan), residents must have an income at least five and a half times the monthly rent—which, depending on the age and location, ranges from fairly low to just below average for private apartments. This means there is a floor below which the income of residents cannot fall, a stipulation that ensures a certain homogeneity. In the case of metropolitan housing, there is an effort to provide homes for people who have resided in the metropolitan area a fixed number of years, who are in housing difficulties, and whose incomes are below a certain level—in this case there is an upper ceiling that again provides a certain homogeneity. In terms of family composition, housing is not for single persons but for those who are currently married or soon to be married. Consideration is given to families with handicapped members and to elderly parents who at the time of application are obliged to reside separately from their children.

2. One tatami mat is approximately 6 feet by 3 feet, but slightly smaller mats called "*danchi* size" have been developed.

3. I define the term "community" in Chapter 2. At this time, I am using the term only to refer to a group outside the family with which the individual identifies and accepts in principle all its obligations and rights.

4. William J. Goode (1973, 97–120) sees role relations as a sequence of "role bargains" in which a person selects certain types of role behavior in order to reduce his or her role strain. Role strain occurs basically because the "individual's total role obligations are overdemanding." Structurally induced moti-

vations are motives that can be derived from knowledge of social structures rather than knowledge about the person; these motivations have to do with occupying a status (Robert K. Merton, lecture, Columbia University, March 19, 1975). I am indebted to Herbert Passin for pointing out the need to distinguish between structurally induced motivations and the variety of structural alternatives presented to occupants of the same status who are subject to the same structurally induced motivations.

An example of a structurally induced motivation would be the motivation of a husband to provide economically for his family (the motivation stems from the status); structural alternatives might include various occupations. For a mother, the structurally induced motivation is to see that her child is well educated; structural alternatives might include PTA, tutoring, etc.

Chapter 2

1. The work of Toennies, Simmel, and Weber, among others, has contributed to this image.

2. The dictionary defines *kyōdōtai* as (1) a binding social relationship or social group which does not recognize individual freedom; (2) the general category of social relationships based on common occupancy of a fixed area of land. Interviewees informed me that they no longer wanted *kyōdōtai* relationships because they restricted their freedom and privacy.

3. These connotations are based on Irokawa (1975), Nakamura (1973, 49–68), and interview data.

4. Irokawa (1975) argues that a three-step migration will occur—from a declining village to temporary urban housing and finally to a new purchased home. When the family is in its permanent home, a community will develop.

5. Although there are no reliable figures (even estimates of the size of these movements vary widely), one nationwide survey indicates that 1.7 percent of the women respondents had at some time been involved in such a movement. (See Fujin ni kansuru 1974, 298.)

6. *Chōnaikai* were officially disbanded in 1944 as part of the postwar decentralization of Japanese government. Shortly afterward, however, in one form or another these associations were revived to meet the needs of police and fire protection as well as other services that the government was not yet able to handle. In Santama City (the research site), the same general tendency was observed. In March 1945 the town council turned to the old *chōnaikai* units to form a Town Police Support Association. After progressive political groups violently protested, the town administration decided to refrain from using former *chōnaikai* to carry out official business. Individual *chōnaikai,* then, revived more or less independently. The Santama City government used the postal services to send notices to residents and placed newsletters in ordinary newspapers. In certain areas, however, *chōnaikai* do act as an extension of the government. For example, they act as fundraising organizations, maintain local street lighting, and help locate people to carry out government surveys. (See Komyunitei Ōganizeishon Kenkyūkai 1976, 40–41.)

7. Interviewees also indicated that this was the case. For example, *chōnai-*

kai meetings were characterized as attended only by the old and by people who had lived in the area for a long time and were not sympathetic to the problems of the young or temporary residents.

8. *Mai hōmu* ("my home") is a Japanized English term that refers to a privately owned residence. One may ask, for example, "Do you live in *mai hōmu?*" meaning "Do you own your own home?"

9. Interviewees defined protection of privacy as the wish to avoid the sticky relations found in the small town or the country.

10. See Keizai Kikakuchō (1975, 11–14). Continuing trends in this direction are pointed out in Kokumin Seikatsu Shingikai (1985).

11. The concept of status indicates not only a person's position in the social system but also the accompanying role set. (See Merton 1968, 422–423.)

12. This statement assumes the woman is a full-time housewife. See, for example, Dore (1958), Vogel (1967), and Wazaki (1965).

Chapter 3

1. See "Nihon josei no sugao o shōkai" (1977). The high marriage rate of Japanese women is also documented in Sōrifu (1983, 27).

2. At the time of the study the Japanese divorce rate was 1.11 per 1,000 persons, which compares with 4.03 for the United States at that time. (See Sōrifu 1978, 118.) Although the rate has since risen to 1.5 per 1,000, it is questionable whether it will continue to rise to match Western figures. As Kumagai (1983) argues, part of the current rate is demographic. As the baby boom divorces abate, the rate will fall. Furthermore, family interaction patterns as well as work options for women argue against a much higher divorce rate.

3. The distinction between a "love marriage" and an "arranged marriage" *(omiai)* is often difficult to make. One may be introduced to someone, fall in love, and decide to marry. Older women are less likely to say they have a love marriage; more often than not, the response is likely to be "we just fell into marriage."

4. See Pharr (1981) and Lebra (1976a). Pharr refers to the three types as neotraditionalists, new women, and radical egalitarians. Lebra uses terms emphasizing the division of labor: dimorphic, bimorphic, and amorphic.

5. See Rōdōshō Fujin Shonen Kyoku (1975, 187); the data are from a national survey published in 1974. See also Fujin ni kansuru (1974, 98).

6. See Sōrifu (1978, 175); the data are from a 1976 national survey of women aged twenty and above. In 1983, Sōrifu (1983, 158) reported 33.2 percent clearly agreeing with the traditional position and an additional 37.9 percent indicating weaker agreement.

7. For a description of housewives' political activity, see Pharr (1981). For a description of the nationwide spread of consumer workshops and the screening of applicants by tests, see "Shizuka na būmu tsuzuku" (1978).

8. "Status competition" refers to the case in which two or more statuses compete for the limited time and energy of the status occupant (Robert K. Merton, lecture, Columbia University, March 26, 1975)—for example, the

mother who is a member of the PTA may find these two statuses compete for her time. "Status conflict" refers to the situation in which the normative demands of the statuses conflict—being a physician, for example, demands that one give first consideration to one's patients whereas being a mother demands that one give first consideration to one's family.

9. See the series *Shufu ga shūgyo suru toki* [When housewives go to work], which appeared from time to time in the *Nihon Keizai Shinbun* in 1978.

10. According to Pharr (1981), some people objected that women are biologically weaker than men and such activity would therefore exhaust them.

11. The following discussion is based on Vogel (1978, 24–35). See also Caudill and Weinstein (1974) and DeVos (1973).

12. According to Kiyohara (1978, 66–67), the Katei Bunko (home library) movement is composed of women who either form a small group and meet in the home of one member who has space to keep children's books (meetings are held once a week for a couple of hours during which the children who are members can borrow and return books and women take turns reading stories, playing games, etc., with the children) or join a larger group to engage in the same activities but make use of the facilities of some community hall or the like to store books and meet (this is usually called *chiiki bunko* or "regional library").

Chapter 4

1. To investigate the question of community for urban Japanese house-wives, I decided to study the relative effect of residence milieu, which I sub-divided into two areas: the issue of owning versus renting and the relevance of housing type. I then divided housing into five categories: *danchi,* company housing, housing rented from private owners, personally owned condomin-iums, and personally owned homes. This division is not exhaustive, as there are people who rent condominiums, purchase apartments in *danchi,* live above their shops, or reside with their parents. For the purposes of a pilot study that could be handled by a single researcher, however, I decided to limit the scope to these five categories.

My basic assumption was that each category has its own social structure, which leads to a social perspective for its occupants. Each category, I hypothe-sized, may place certain constraints on its residents or create certain options for them and lead to different perceptions of their community and their partic-ipation in its activities. For example, company employees living in housing with the husband's superiors may find that the wives of superiors influence the activity of junior wives.

2. Unless otherwise cited, all data come from government statistics on San-tama City.

3. The original plan was not well thought out. It was assumed that the city government would simply turn over the building and a fixed sum of money to elected representatives of the residents. It was soon discovered, however, that problems arose in regard to management of public funds, and now the city sends an employee to each community center to manage the money. This

employee's function is not to decide how to spend the funds but to help the residents realize as many of their plans as possible with the funds available.

4. "Circle," an English word adopted into Japanese, refers to an activity group—for example, paper-flower-making circles and book-reading circles.

5.

Annual Family Income of Respondent

Income	Survey		Interviews	
(unit = 1,000,000 yen)	Percent	Number	Percent	Number
2.5 or less	19.3%	44	8%	4
2.55–4.00	27.2	62	30	15
4.05–5.00	15.8	36	20	10
5.05–6.00	10.1	23	10	5
6.05–7.00	3.9	9	4	2
7.05–8.00	4.4	10	8	4
over 8.00	5.2	12	2	1
DK/NA	14.0	32	18	9
	100%	228	100%	50

6. Women who indicated that they themselves *believed* in one of the established traditional sects such as True Pure Land Buddhism (Jōdō Shinshū) were classified as believers in Buddhism. Those who indicated belief in one of the groups commonly referred to as Shinkō Shūkyō ("New Religions") such as Sōka Gakkai were placed in this category. Although the New Religions may have a history of more than a hundred years and some of the sects deny they are New Religions, their proselytizing activity as well as their appeal to individual faith sets them apart from traditional sects. The latter are, in general, characterized as the "family religion" regardless of individual belief. Involvement in such religions consists for the most part in funeral and memorial rites.

Chapter 5

1. This discussion is based on Lopata (1971). I use the term "life course" throughout this study to avoid the implication that each new cohort repeats the exact pattern of the previous one.

2. "Honorary go-betweens" are persons who have not actually introduced the couple but are somehow related to their future (the husband's boss or university professor, for example) or to the prosperity of the family (an actual or potential benefactor) or a person of stature. By fulfilling the role of go-between in the marriage ceremony, they not only fill a blank space in the ceremony but theoretically give the couple an advisor. Go-betweens should also be at least middle-aged so that their own marriage can serve as a model.

3. By virtue of her turn as a member of her *danchi* association, for example, one woman was representing that *danchi* at the local community center.

4. See Sōrifu (1978, 41). In 1980, some 49.4 percent of women were in the labor force; of these, 66.7 percent were married (Sōrifu 1983, 70–71).

5. See Sōrifu (1978, 45). By 1980 the top of the second peak had become much flatter, reflecting women's increasing labor-force participation.

6. The figures are for 1978 and are based on "Gekizo suru naishoku sōdan" (1978).

7. A different opinion was expressed by staff at a nursery for children of working mothers. They felt that the husbands of working mothers tended to help with the more conspicuous tasks (those that would be noticed in the neighborhood) such as hanging out bedding or sweeping the walk, leaving all the inside work to their wives.

8. At the time of the study, more than 60 percent of both samples were not in the labor force. *Naishoku* accounted for 6 percent of the survey sample and 4 percent of the interviewees. An additional 10 percent (survey) and 8 percent (interview) were involved in the family business. Only 5 percent of those surveyed and no interviewees were employed full time, whereas 4 percent surveyed and 8 percent interviewed worked part time. In addition, 6 percent surveyed and 12 percent interviewed were engaged in skilled, semiprofessional, or professional occupations.

9. A regional women's group is one that all women living in a district *(chiiki)* may join. Activities are up to the group itself. Currently such groups tend to be composed of older women, and many have trouble recruiting new members.

10. See Kiefer (1974, 18ff.). Morioka (1968, 237), however, points out that the characteristics of *danchi* residents are not unique but apply to all white-collar residents regardless of residence type.

11. Whereas 35.4 percent of those with preschool children lived in their own homes (houses), the figure rose to 52.5 percent for those with elementary school children, 64.2 percent for those with junior high and high school children, and 88.5 percent for those with children in college. Then it dropped slightly to 78.4 percent for those with adult children.

Chapter 6

1. Babysitters are not cheap. The lowest fee for babysitting I heard of was 400 yen per hour as a student part-time job. This is roughly equivalent to the hourly wage a housewife would earn from part-time work.

2. The average annual income for an employed individual in 1975 was 2.2 million yen. In 1980, the average household income was 5.09 million yen.

3. The Children's Theater is not a Santama City organization but has branches throughout the nation.

4. Vanek (1980, 280) points out that a similar situation exists in the United States: Husbands perform the "feminine tasks" grudgingly or ineptly, and wives are "reluctant to relinquish primary responsibility for the household."

5. The issue of rationalization of housework in the West is taken up by Glazer (1980, 258–259).

6. Ferree (1980, 105) hypothesizes that social isolation may be voluntary

for women whose children are in school and involuntary for those with small children.

Chapter 7

1. This relationship supports Litwak's argument about the various functions of primary groups. (See Chapter 6.)

Chapter 8

1. "Old country" relations refer to the expectation that neighbors will help one another with various activities and emergencies. These relations not only involve a great deal of mutual visibility but also limit one's personal freedom to deviate from customary patterns of behavior.

2. The question of privacy is of course a personal matter. For some people, privacy means secrecy; others prefer more openness. When interviewees referred to privacy they were talking about the visibility of their families, how they spent their money, what possessions they had, and so forth. The issue was usually one of family privacy, not individual privacy.

3. Although this is not necessarily true, it could become a self-fulfilling prophecy.

4. The Asahi Culture Center is a private institution which offers a wide variety of courses, primarily to housewives.

5. "Nonrequired groups" include those devoted to study, leisure, child or family matters, social service, consumer affairs, the community, and politics.

6. The Children's Theater is a nationwide group. Members pay fees and purchase discount tickets for a certain number of performances a year. There are block and district branches with volunteer members circulating newsletters, collecting dues, and commenting on past performances and future requests. They also have other activities such as a summer camp for children.

7. This information supports the findings of Kiyohara (1978).

Chapter 10

1. In this context, "circle" also refers to social service, civic, and other activities.

2. Here the assumption is that the husband's work does not depend on neighbors as clients.

Select Bibliography

Abegglen, James C.
   1973   *Management and Worker: The Japanese Solution.* Tokyo: Sophia University Press.

Agora
   1977   "Agora teichiin: Naze shōgai kyōiku o tema ni suru no?" [Agora teach-in: Why do we take the theme of lifelong education?]. *Agora* 17 (November 20): 39–50.

"Anke-to no matome: Kosodate-ki no shufu no seikatsu: Hito to no kakawari o chūshin ni" [Survey results: The life of housewives during the child-rearing period: Focus on interpersonal relations]
   1979   *Waifu* [Wife] 156 (February): 32–40.

Aoi, Kazuo, and Kōkichi Masuda, eds.
   1973   *Kazoku hendō no shakaigaku* [Sociology of family change]. Tokyo: Baifukan.

Asukada, Kazuo, ed.
   1965   *Jichitai kaikaku no rironteki tenbō* [Theoretical perspective on the reform of self-governing associations]. Tokyo: Nihon Hyōronsha.

Berger, Michael
   1976   "Japanese Women—Old Images and New Realities." *Japan Interpreter* 11: 56–67.

Berk, Sarah Fenstermaker, ed.
   1980   *Women and Household Labor.* Vol. 5, Sage Yearbooks in Women's Policy Studies. Beverly Hills: Sage Publications.

Bestor, Theodore C.
   1985   "Tradition and Japanese Social Organization: Institutional Development in a Tokyo Neighborhood." *Ethnology* 25: 121–135.

Boranteia Kenkyūkai [Research Group on Volunteers], ed.
   1976   *Nihon no boranteia fukushi shakai e no shuppatsu ten* [Japanese volunteers: The departure point to a welfare society]. Tokyo: Zenkoku Shakai Fukushi Kyōgikai [National Council on Social Welfare].

Caudill, William, and Helen Weinstein
    1974   "Maternal Care and Infant Behavior in Japan and America." In *Japanese Culture and Behavior: Selected Readings,* ed. Takie Sugiyama Lebra and William P. Lebra. Honolulu: University Press of Hawaii.

"Chōsa ripōto: Kekkon no jigakuzō: Anata wa, ima doko ni iru no ka?" [Research report: A map of marital consciousness: Where are you now?]
    1977   *Watakushi wa onna* [I am woman] 1 (5): 63–102.

Cole, Robert E.
    1971   *Japanese Blue Collar: The Changing Tradition.* Berkeley and Los Angeles: University of California Press.

"Danchi no josei wa iyoku tappuri" [*Danchi* women are full of eagerness]
    1978   *Asahi Shimbun,* May 3.

DeVos, George A.
    1973   *Socialization for Achievement: Essays on the Cultural Psychology of the Japanese.* Berkeley and Los Angeles: University of California Press.

Dore, Ronald P.
    1958   *City Life in Japan. A Study of a Tokyo Ward.* Berkeley and Los Angeles: University of California Press.

Effrat, Marcia Pelly, ed.
    1974   *The Community: Approaches and Applications.* New York: Free Press.

Epstein, Cynthia Fuchs
    1970   *Woman's Place: Options and Limits in Professional Careers.* Berkeley and Los Angeles: University of California Press.

Fava, Sylvia F.
    1978   "Women's Place in the New Suburbia." Unpublished manuscript.

Fellin, Phillip, and Eugene Litwak
    1968   "The Neighborhood in Urban American Society." *Social Work* (July): 72–80.

Ferree, Myra Marx
    1980   "Satisfaction with Housework: The Social Context." In *Women and Household Labor,* ed. Sarah Berk. Beverly Hills: Sage Publications.

Festinger, Leon, Stanley Schachter, and Kurt Back
    1950   *Social Pressures in Informal Groups: A Study of Human Factors in Housing.* Stanford: Stanford University Press.

Foreign Press Center of Japan
    1977   *The Women of Japan—Past and Present.* About Japan Series No. 5 (July).

Fujin ni kansuru shomondai chōsakaigi [Council for Investigating Women's Problems], ed.
    1974   *Gendai nihon josei no ishiki to kōdō: Fujin ni kansuru shomondai no*

sōgō chōsa hōkokusho [The mentality and behavior of contemporary Japanese women: Report of a comprehensive survey on various women's issues]. Tokyo: Ōkurasho Insatsu-kyoku [Finance Ministry Press].

Fuse, Akiko
1967 "Toshi kazoku no naibu kōzō no hen' yo ni kansuru 1 kōsatsu: (Shokugyō o motsu shufu) no kazoku to (shufu sengyō no shufu) no kazoku no hikaku" [A study on changes in the internal structure of the urban family: A comparison between the families of working wives and full-time housewives]. *Shakaigaku Hyōron* 17 (4): 45–71.

1978 "The State and Problems of Housewives' Work in Contemporary Japan." In *Proceedings of the Tokyo Symposium on Women.* Tokyo: International Group for the Study of Women.

Gans, Herbert J.
1962a *The Levittowners: Ways of Life and Politics in a New Suburban Community.* New York: Random House.

1962b *The Urban Villagers: Group and Class in the Life of Italian-Americans.* New York: Free Press.

"Gekizō suru naishoku sōdan" [Increasing counseling on piecework at home]
1978 *Asahi Shimbun,* April 18.

Gerth, H. H., and C. Wright Mills, eds.
1946 *From Max Weber: Essays in Sociology.* New York: Oxford University Press.

Glazer, Nona
1980 "Everyone Needs Three Hands: Doing Unpaid and Paid Work." In *Women and Household Labor,* ed. Sarah Berk. Beverly Hills: Sage Publications.

Goode, William J.
1970 *World Revolution and Family Patterns.* New York: Free Press.

1973 *Explorations in Social Theory.* New York: Oxford University Press.

Higuchi, Keiko
1975 "The PTA—A Channel for Political Activism." *Japan Interpreter* 10 (2): 133–140.

"Himatsubushi de wa arimasen: Josei no shōgai kyōiku jūkō-netsu" [It is not just a way to kill time: Women's fervid interest in lifelong education]
1978 *Nihon Keizai Shinbun,* July 14.

Hunter, Albert
1974 *Symbolic Communities: The Persistence and Change of Chicago's Local Communities.* Chicago: University of Chicago Press.

"Ie ni ikigai toppu: Hataraku fujin no chōsa shokugyō ni angai shosu" [The family comes out top as source of meaning in life: Survey of working married women reveals unexpectedly small differences by type of employment]
1977 *Asahi Shimbun,* October 19.

Iga, Mitsuya
   1978   "Fujin shūgyō no shūkiteki henka to rekishiteki henka" [Cyclical and
           historical changes in women's work]. *Shakaigaku Hyōron* 29 (3):
           27–56.

Irokawa, Daikichi
   1975   "The Survival Struggle of the Japanese Community." *Japan Inter-
           preter* 4 (9): 466–494.

Iwao, Sumiko
   n.d.   "A Full Life for Modern Japanese Women." *Text of Seminar Chang-
           ing Values in Modern Japan.* Nihonjin Kenkyūkai [Research Group
           on the Japanese].
   1976   "Onna no manzokukan—onna no ikigai" [Women's satisfaction—
           women's meaning in life]. In *Nihonjin, Kenkyū No. 3; Tokushū:
           Onna ga kangaete iru koto* [The Japanese, research no. 3; special
           topic: What women are thinking], ed. Nihonjin Kenkyūkai [Re-
           search Group on the Japanese]. Tokyo: Taiseidō.

Janeway, Elizabeth
   1971   *Man's World, Woman's Place: A Study in Social Mythology.* New
           York: Penguin Books.

Kamishima, Jirō
   1961   *Kindai Nihon no seishin kōzō* [The structure of the modern Japanese
           spirit]. Tokyo: Miraisha.

Kasamatsu, Keiichi, ed.
   1973   *Danchi no Subete* [All about *danchi*]. Tokyo: Seikatsu Kagaku Chō-
           sakai.

Katz, Elihu, and Paul F. Lazarsfeld
   1955   *Personal Influence: The Part Played by People in the Flow of Mass
           Communications.* New York: Free Press.

Keizai Kikakuchō [Economic Planning Agency], ed.
   1975   *Komyunitei to kurashi no kankyō—jumin sanka no machizukuri*
           [Community and living environment—town-building with residents'
           participation]. Tokyo: Ōkurasho Insatsu Kyoku [Finance Ministry
           Press].
   1976   *Shōwa 51 nen han: Kokumin seikatsu hakushō—kurashi no naka no
           atarashii teiryū* [1976 edition: White paper on national life—a new
           undercurrent in daily life]. Tokyo: Ōkurasho Insatsu Kyoku [Finance
           Ministry Press].
   1977   *Shōwa 52 nen han: Kokumin seikatsu hakushō* [1977 edition: White
           paper on national life]. Tokyo: Ōkurasho Insatsu Kyoku [Finance
           Ministry Press].

Kiefer, Christie W.
   1968   "Personality and Social Change in a Japanese Danchi." Ph.D. disser-
           tation, University of California, Berkeley.

1974 "The Danchi Zoku and the Evolution of the Metropolitan Mind." In *Japan: The Paradox of Progress*, ed. Lewis Austin. New Haven: Yale University Press.

Kinoshita, Ritsuko
1983 *Ōkoku no Tsumatachi: Kigyō Jōkamachi Nite.* [Wives of the kingdom: The company castle town]. Tokyo: Komichi Shōbō.

Kiyohara, Keiko
1977 Toshi no shufu no hōsō riyō—gakushū ni kansuru ichi kōsatsu [Urban housewives' radio use—a small study in learning]. In *Shinbun Kenkyūsho nenpō* [Annual report of the Newspaper Research Institute]. Keiō Gijuku Daigaku Shinbun Kenkyūsho [Keio University Newpaper Research Institute] 9:73–93.

1978 "Chiiki shakai to shakai kyōiku—bunkō katsudō no tenkai to shufu no ishiki henka o meguru ichi jitsurei kenkyū" [Local society and social education—a case study illustrating the development of the home library movement and changes in housewives' consciousness]. *Shakaigaku Kenkyū-ka Kiyō* [Sociology Research Department Bulletin] 18:65–73.

Kokubunji Shiritsu Honda Kōminkan
1977 Fujin mondai kōza [Symposium on women's issues]. *Shōwa 52 seijin kōza no kiroku: Sazanami* [Records of adult education 1977]. Kokubunji City.

Kokumin Seikatsu Shingikai Sōgō Seisakubukai Chōsa Iinkai [Research Steering Committee of the Comprehensive Policy Section of the Deliberative Assembly on National Life], ed.
1985 *Kokumin Seikatsu Shihyō—NSI* [New social indicators]. Tokyo: Ōkurasho Insatsu Kyoku [Finance Ministry Press].

Komarovsky, Mirra
1962 *Blue-Collar Marriage.* New York: Vintage Books.

Komyunitei Ōganizeishon Kenkyūkai [Research Association on Community Organization]
1976 *Hoken fukushi no ryoiki ni okeru komyunitei ōganizeishon ni kansuru kenkyū dai 3ji hōkoku-sho* [Research on community organization within welfare insurance third stage report]. Tokyo.

"Komyunitei sentā sararīman mo katsuyō o" [Salarymen too use community centers]
1978 *Nihon Keizai Shinbun,* January 8.

Koyano, Shōgo
1978 "Thought Patterns and Their Change Among the Collective Housing Dwellers in Tokyo." Unpublished manuscript.

Kumagai, Fumie
1983 "Changing Divorce in Japan." *Journal of Family History* 8 (1): 85–108.

Kunitachi Shi Kōminkan Shimin Daigaku Seminā no Kiroku [Records of the Kunitachi City Public Hall Adult Education Seminar]
1977 *Shufu to onna* [Housewife and woman]. Tokyo: Miraisha.

Lebra, Joyce, et al., eds.
1976 *Women in Changing Japan*. Boulder: Westview Press.

Lebra, Takie Sugiyama
1976a "Sex Equality for Japanese Women." *Japan Interpreter* 10 (3–4): 284–295.
1976b *Japanese Patterns of Behavior*. Honolulu: University Press of Hawaii.
1984 *Japanese Women: Constraint and Fulfillment*. Honolulu: University of Hawaii Press.

Lebra, Takie Sugiyama, and William P. Lebra, eds.
1974 *Japanese Culture and Behavior: Selected Readings*. Honolulu: University Press of Hawaii.

Litwak, Eugene, and Josefina Figueira
1968 "Technical Innovation and Theoretical Function of Primary Groups and Bureaucratic Structures." *American Journal of Sociology* 73 (4): 468–481.

Litwak, Eugene, and Ivan Szelenyi
1969 "Primary Group Structures and Their Functions: Kin, Neighbors, and Friends." *American Sociological Review* 34 (4): 465–481.

Lopata, Helena Z.
1971 *Occupation: Housewife*. London: Oxford University Press.

McKean, Margaret Anne
1981 *Environmental Protest and Citizen Politics in Japan*. Berkeley and Los Angeles: University of California Press.

Mainichi Shinbunsha Kōbe Shikyoku
1977 *Toshi to shufu tachi: Kōbe shi Fujin Dantai Kyōgikai no ayumi* [The city and housewives: The progress of the Kobe Council of Women's Associations]. Tokyo: Mainichi Shinbunsha.

Matsubara, Haruo
1971 "Chiiki shūkai no keisei to jūmin undō" [The formation of local meetings and residents' movements]. In *Toshi keisei to ronri to jūmin* [City planning, theory and residents], ed. Isomura Eiichi et al. Tokyo: Tōkyō Daigaku Shuppankai [Tokyo University Press].

Merton, Robert K.
1968 *Social Theory and Social Structure*. New York: Free Press.

Michelson, William
1974 "The Reconciliation of 'Subjective' and 'Objective' Data on Physical Environment in the Community: The Case of Social Contact in High-Rise Apartments." In *The Community: Approaches and Applications*, ed. Marcia Pelly Effrat. New York: Free Press.

Morgan, Maribel
1975 *The Total Woman.* Old Tappan, N.J.: Revell.

Morioka, Kiyomi
1968 "Tōkyō kinkō danchi kazoku no seikatsu shi to shakai sanka" [Social participation and life histories of families in Tokyo suburban *danchi*]. *Kokusai Kirisuto Daigaku Gakuhō Shakai Kagaku Jānaru* [International Christian University Social Science Journal] II B (7): 199–277.

Nakamura, Hachirō
1973 *Toshi komyunitei no shakaigaku* [Urban community sociology]. Tokyo: Yūhikaku.

"Nihon josei no sugao o shōkai" [Introducing the real face of Japanese women]
1977 *Asahi Shimbun,* October 21.

Oakley, Ann
1974 *The Sociology of Housework.* New York: Pantheon Books.

Ogburn, William F.
1963 "The Changing Functions of the Family." In *Selected Studies in Marriage and the Family,* ed. R. F. Winch et al. New York: Holt, Rinehart and Winston.

Ōhara, Shin
1976 *Onna, kodomo, komyunitei* [Women, children, community]. Tokyo: PHP Kenkyūsho.

Okuda, Michihirō
1977 "Toshi kazoku to komyunitei—'mai komyunitei' fūkei no mondaisei" [Urban families and community—problems with the "my community" landscape]. In *Jūrisuto: Zōkan, sōgō tokushū gendai no kazoku* [The jurist: Special issue on the contemporary family] (6): 115–121.

"Onna, koko ni ikite dai 4 kai: Jishin to tomodachi o hagukunda 5 nenkan no dokushokai katsudō" [Women, find your life here—number 4: Five-year active participation in a reading circle cherishing self and friends]
1979 *Asahi Katei Benrichō '79* 4 (April 1): 2–3.

"Otoko wa shigoto, onna wa katei: Sansei wa 20% dake" [Men work and women mind the home: Only 20% in favor]
1978 *Asahi Shimbun,* September 18.

Ōyabu, Jūichi
1975a "Danchi: Nagaya to hoteru" [*Danchi:* Long house and hotel]. *Asahi Shimbun,* November 19.
1975b "Danchi: Furusato" [*Danchi:* Hometown]. *Asahi Shimbun,* November 21.

Pahl, J. M., and R. E. Pahl
1971 *Managers and Their Wives: A Study of Career and Family Relationships in the Middle Class.* Middlesex, England: Penguin Books.

Perry, Linda Louise
  1976 "Mothers, Wives and Daughters in Osaka: Autonomy, Alliance, and Professionalism." Ph.D. diss., University of Pittsburgh.

Pharr, Susan J.
  1981 *Political Women in Japan.* Berkeley and Los Angeles: University of California Press.

Rapoport, Rhona, and Robert Rapoport
  1971 *Dual Career Families.* Middlesex, England: Penguin Books.

Rōdōshō Fujin Shonen Kyoku [Ministry of Labor Bureau on Women and Children], ed.
  1975 *Fujin no ayumi 30 nen* [Thirty years of women's progress]. Tokyo: Rōdō Hōrei Kyōkai [Labor Law Society].

Rohlen, Thomas P.
  1974 *For Harmony and Strength: Japanese White-Collar Organization in Anthropological Perspective.* Berkeley and Los Angeles: University of California Press.

Salamon, Sonya
  1975 "The Varied Group of Japanaese and German Housewives." *Japan Interpreter* 10 (2): 151–170.

Shadan Hōjin: Shakai Kaihatsu Tōkei Kenkyūsho [Research Agency on Social Development Statistics]
  1975 *Komyunitei jūmin ishiki chōsa hōkoku-shō* [Report on community resident consciousness]. Tokyo: Shadan Hōjin: Shakai Kaihatsu Tōkei Kenkyūsho.

Sharpe, Sue
  1976 *Just Like a Girl: How Girls Learn to Be Women.* New York: Penguin Books.

Shills, Edward A.
  1952 "The Study of the Primary Group." In *The Policy Sciences' Recent Developments in Scope and Method,* eds. Daniel Lerner and Harold D. Lasswell. Stanford: Stanford University Press.

"Shizuka na būmu tsuzuku" [The quiet boom continues]
  1978 *Nihon Keizai Shinbun,* June 30.

Sōrifu [Prime Minister's Office], ed.
  1978 *Fujin no genjō to shisaku (Kokunai Kōdō Keikaku Dai ikai hōkoku-shō)* [The present life conditions of women and governmental policies: The first report on the National Action Program]. Tokyo: Gyōsei.

  1983 *Fujin no genjō to shisaku (Kokunai Kōdō Keikaku Dai sankai hōkoku-shō)* [The present life conditions of women and governmental policies: The third report on the National Action Program]. Tokyo: Gyōsei.

Stinchcombe, Arthur I.
1976 "Merton's Theory of Social Structure." In *The Idea of Social Structure: Papers in Honor of Robert K. Merton,* ed. Lewis A. Coser. New York: Harcourt Brace Jovanovich.

Suttles, Gerald D.
1972 *The Social Construction of Communities.* Chicago: University of Chicago Press.

Takabatake, Michitoshi
1973 "Ima undō ni nani ga towarete-iru ka" [What issues are currently being raised in social movements?]. *Ushio* (September): 87–91.
1975 "Citizens' Movements: Organizing the Spontaneous." *Japan Interpreter* 9 (3): 315–323.

Taki, Ikuko
1976 *Danchi Mama no Funsen Ki* [A record of the struggles of a *danchi* mother]. Tokyo: Shin Nihon Shinshō 218.

Tiryakian, Edward A., ed.
1963 *Sociological Theory, Values, and Sociocultural Change.* Glencoe, Ill.: Free Press.

Toennies, Ferdinand
1957 *Community and Society.* Trans. and ed. Charles P. Loomis. New York: Harper & Row.

Vanek, Joann
1980 "Household Work, Wage Work, and Sexual Equality." In *Women and Household Labor,* ed. Sarah Berk. Beverly Hills: Sage Publications.

Vogel, Ezra F.
1967 *Japan's New Middle Class: The Salary Man and His Family in a Tokyo Suburb.* Berkeley and Los Angeles: University of California Press.

Vogel, Suzanne H.
1978 "Professional Housewife: The Career of Urban Middle Class Japanese Women." *Japan Interpreter* 12 (1): 16–43.

Wazaki, Hōichi
1965 "Chiiki shakai no kenkyū" [Research on local society]. *Jinbun Gakuhō* 21:153–174.

Whyte, William H., Jr.
1956 *The Organization Man.* New York: Simon & Schuster.

Yoshida, Noboru, and Michiko Kanda, eds.
1977 *Gendai josei no ishiki to seikatsu* [Modern women's mentality and life]. Tokyo: NHK Bukusu 237.

Index

Studies of the
East Asian Institute

The Ladder of Success in Imperial China. Ping-ti Ho. New York: Columbia University Press, 1962.

The Chinese Inflation, 1937–1949. Shun-hsin Chou. New York: Columbia University Press, 1963.

Reformer in Modern China: Chang Chien, 1853–1926. Samuel Chu. New York: Columbia University Press, 1965.

Research in Japanese Sources: A Guide. Herschel Webb, with the assistance of Marleigh Ryan. New York: Columbia University Press, 1965.

Society and Education in Japan. Herbert Passin. New York: Teachers College Press, 1965.

Agricultural Production and Economic Development in Japan, 1873–1922. James I. Nakamura. Princeton: Princeton University Press, 1966.

Japan's First Modern Novel: Ukigumo of Futabatei Shimei. Marleigh Ryan. New York: Columbia University Press, 1967.

The Korean Communist Movement, 1918–1948. Dae-Sook Suh. Princeton: Princeton University Press, 1967.

The First Vietnam Crisis. Melvin Gurtov. New York: Columbia University Press, 1967.

Cadres, Bureaucracy and Political Power in Communist China. A. Doak Barnett. New York: Columbia University Press, 1968.

The Japanese Imperial Institution in the Tokugawa Period. Herschel Webb. New York: Columbia University Press, 1968.

Higher Education and Business Recruitment in Japan. Koya Azumi. New York: Columbia University Press, 1969.

The Communists and Peasant Rebellions: A Study in the Rewriting of Chinese History. James P. Harrison, Jr. New York: Atheneum, 1969.

How the Conservatives Rule Japan. Nathaniel B. Thayer. Princeton: Princeton University Press, 1969.

Aspects of Chinese Education. C. T. Hu, ed. New York: Teachers College Press, 1970.

Documents of Korean Communism, 1918–1948. Dae-Sook Suh. Princeton: Princeton University Press, 1970.

Japanese Education: A Bibliography of Materials in the English Language. Herbert Passin. New York: Teachers College Press, 1970.

Economic Development and the Labor Market in Japan. Koji Taira. New York: Columbia University Press, 1970.

The Japanese Oligarchy and the Russo-Japanese War. Shumpei Okamoto. New York: Columbia University Press, 1970.

Imperial Restoration in Medieval Japan. H. Paul Varley. New York: Columbia University Press, 1971.

Japan's Postwar Defense Policy, 1947–1968. Martin E. Weinstein. New York: Columbia University Press, 1971.

Election Campaigning Japanese Style. Gerald L. Curtis. New York: Columbia University Press, 1971.

China and Russia: The "Great Game." O. Edmund Clubb. New York: Columbia University Press, 1971.

Money and Monetary Policy in Communist China. Katharine Huang Hsiao. New York: Columbia University Press, 1971.

The District Magistrate in Late Imperial China. John R. Watt. New York: Columbia University Press, 1972.

Law and Policy in China's Foreign Relations: A Study of Attitudes and Practice. James C. Hsiung. New York: Columbia University Press, 1972.

Pearl Harbor as History: Japanese-American Relations, 1931–1941. Dorothy Borg and Shumpei Okamoto, eds., with the assistance of Dale K. A. Finlayson. New York: Columbia University Press, 1973.

Japanese Culture: A Short History. H. Paul Varley. New York: Praeger, 1973.

Doctors in Politics: The Political Life of the Japan Medical Association. William E. Steslicke. New York: Praeger, 1973.

The Japan Teachers Union: A Radical Interest Group in Japanese Politics. Donald Ray Thurston. Princeton: Princeton University Press, 1973.

Japan's Foreign Policy, 1868–1941: A Research Guide. James William Morley, ed. New York: Columbia University Press, 1974.

Palace and Politics in Prewar Japan. David Anson Titus. New York: Columbia University Press, 1974.

The Idea of China: Essays in Geographic Myth and Theory. Andrew March. Devon, England: David and Charles, 1974.

Origins of the Cultural Revolution. Roderick MacFarquhar. New York: Columbia University Press, 1974.

Shiba Kokan: Artist, Innovator, and Pioneer in the Westernization of Japan. Calvin L. French. Tokyo: Weatherhill, 1974.

Insei: Abdicated Sovereigns in the Politics of Late Heian Japan. G. Cameron Hurst. New York: Columbia University Press, 1975.

Embassy at War. Harold Joyce Noble. Frank Baldwin, Jr., ed. and intro. Seattle: University of Washington Press, 1975.

Rebels and Bureaucrats: China's December 9ers. John Israel and Donald W. Klein. Berkeley: University of California Press, 1975.

Deterrent Diplomacy. James William Morley, ed. New York: Columbia University Press, 1976.

House United, House Divided: The Chinese Family in Taiwan. Myron L. Cohen. New York: Columbia University Press, 1976.

Escape from Predicament: Neo-Confucianism and China's Evolving Political Culture. Thomas A. Metzger. New York: Columbia University Press, 1976.

Cadres, Commanders, and Commissars: The Training of the Chinese Communist Leadership, 1920–45. Jane L. Price. Boulder, Colo.: Westview Press, 1976.

Sun Yat-Sen: Frustrated Patriot. C. Martin Wilbur. New York: Columbia University Press, 1977.

Japanese International Negotiating Style. Michael Blaker. New York: Columbia University Press, 1977.

Contemporary Japanese Budget Politics. John Creighton Campbell. Berkeley: University of California Press, 1977.

The Medieval Chinese Oligarchy. David Johnson. Boulder, Colo.: Westview Press, 1977.

The Arms of Kiangnan: Modernization in the Chinese Ordnance Industry, 1860–1895. Thomas L. Kennedy. Boulder, Colo.: Westview Press, 1978.

Patterns of Japanese Policymaking: Experiences from Higher Education. T. J. Pempel. Boulder, Colo.: Westview Press, 1978.

The Chinese Connection: Roger S. Greene, Thomas W. Lamont, George E. Sokolsky, and American–East Asian Relations. Warren I. Cohen. New York: Columbia University Press, 1978.

Militarism in Modern China: The Career of Wu P'ei-Fu, 1916–1939. Odoric Y. K. Wou. Folkestone, England: Dawson, 1978.

A Chinese Pioneer Family: The Lins of Wu-Feng. Johanna Meskill. Princeton: Princeton University Press, 1979.

Perspectives on a Changing China. Joshua A. Fogel and William T. Rowe, eds. Boulder, Colo.: Westview Press, 1979.

The Memoirs of Li Tsung-Jen. T. K. Tong and Li Tsung-Jen. Boulder, Colo.: Westview Press, 1979.

Unwelcome Muse: Chinese Literature in Shanghai and Peking, 1937–1945. Edward Gunn. New York: Columbia University Press, 1979.

Yenan and the Great Powers: The Origins of Chinese Communist Foreign Policy. James Reardon-Anderson. New York: Columbia University Press, 1980.

190

Uncertain Years: Chinese-American Relations, 1947–1950. Dorothy Borg and Waldo Heinrichs, eds. New York: Columbia University Press, 1980.

The Fateful Choice: Japan's Advance into South-East Asia. James William Morley, ed. New York: Columbia University Press, 1980.

Tanaka Giichi and Japan's China Policy. William F. Morton. Folkestone, England: Dawson, 1980; New York: St. Martin's Press, 1980.

The Origins of the Korean War: Liberation and the Emergence of Separate Regimes, 1945–1947. Bruce Cummings, Princeton: Princeton University Press, 1981.

Class Conflict in Chinese Socialism. Richard Curt Kraus. New York: Columbia University Press, 1981.

Education under Mao: Class and Competition in Canton Schools. Jonathan Unger. New York: Columbia University Press, 1982.

Private Academies of Tokugawa Japan. Richard Rubinger. Princeton: Princeton University Press, 1982.

Japan and the San Francisco Peace Settlement. Michael M. Yoshitsu. New York: Columbia University Press, 1982.

New Frontiers in American–East Asian Relations: Essays Presented to Dorothy Borg. Warren I. Cohen, ed. New York: Columbia University Press, 1983.

The Origins of the Cultural Revolution: II, The Great Leap Forward, 1958–1960. Roderick MacFarquhar. New York: Columbia University Press, 1983.

The China Quagmire: Japan's Expansion on the Asian Continent, 1933–1941. James William Morley, ed. New York: Columbia University Press, 1983.

Fragments of Rainbows: The Life and Poetry of Saito Mokichi, 1882–1953. Amy Vladeck Heinrich. New York: Columbia University Press, 1983.

The U.S.–South Korean Alliance: Evolving Patterns of Security Relations. Gerald L. Curtis and Sung-joo Han, eds. Lexington, Mass.: Lexington Books, 1983.

Japan and the Asian Development Bank. Dennis Yasutomo. New York: Praeger Publishers, 1983.

Discovering History in China: American Historical Writing on the Recent Chinese Past. Paul A. Cohen. New York: Columbia University Press, 1984.

The Foreign Policy of the Republic of Korea. Youngnok Koo and Sungjoo Han, eds. New York: Columbia University Press, 1984.

Japan Erupts: The London Naval Conference and the Manchurian Incident. James W. Morley, ed. New York: Columbia University Press, 1984.

Japanese Culture. 3rd. ed. rev. Paul Varley. Honolulu: University of Hawaii Press, 1984.

Shamans, Housewives, and Other Restless Spirits: Women in Korean Ritual Life. Laurel Kendall. Honolulu: University of Hawaii Press, 1985.

Japan's Modern Myths: Ideology in the Late Meiji Period. Carol Gluck. Princeton: Princeton University Press, 1985.

Human Rights in Contemporary China. R. Randle Edwards, Louis Henkin, and Andrew J. Nathan. New York: Columbia University Press, 1986.

The Pacific Basin: New Challenges for the United States. James W. Morley, ed. New York: The Academy of Political Science, 1986.

The Manner of Giving: Strategic Aid and Japanese Foreign Policy. Dennis T. Yasutomo. Lexington, Mass.: Lexington Books, 1986.

Security Interdependence in the Asia Pacific Region. James W. Morley, ed. Lexington, Mass.: Lexington Books, 1986.

China's Political Economy: The Quest for Development Since 1949. Carl Riskin. New York: Oxford University Press, 1986.

Anvil of Victory: The Communist Revolution in Manchuria. Steven Levine. New York: Columbia University Press, 1987.

Urban Japanese Housewives: At Home and in the Community, by Anne E. Imamura. Honolulu: University of Hawaii Press, 1987.

China's Satellite Parties, by James D. Seymour. Armonk, NY: M. E. Sharpe, 1987.

The Japanese Way of Politics, by Gerald L. Curtis. New York: Columbia University Press, 1988.

Border Crossings: Studies in International History, by Christopher Thorne. Oxford & New York: Basil Blackwell, 1988.

The Indochina Tangle: China's Vietnam Policy, 1975–1979, by Robert S. Ross. New York: Columbia University Press, 1988.

Remaking Japan: The American Occupation as New Deal, by Theodore Cohen, edited by Herbert Passin. New York: The Free Press, 1987.

Kim Il Sung: The North Korean Leader, by Dae-Sook Suh. New York: Columbia University Press, 1988.

Japan and the World, 1853–1952: A Bibliographic Guide to Recent Scholarship in Japanese Foreign Relations, by Sadao Asada. New York: Columbia University Press, 1988.

Contending Approaches to the Political Economy of Taiwan, edited by Edwin A. Winckler and Susan Greenhalgh. Armonk, NY: M. E. Sharpe, 1988.

Aftermath of War: Americans and the Remaking of Japan, 1945–1952, by Howard B. Schonberger. Kent, OH: Kent State University Press, 1989.

Single Sparks: China's Rural Revolutions, edited by Kathleen Hartford and Steven M. Goldstein. Armonk, NY: M. E. Sharpe, 1989.

Neighborhood Tokyo, by Theodore C. Bestor. Stanford: Stanford University Press, 1989.

Missionaries of the Revolution: Soviet Advisers and Chinese Nationalism, by

C. Martin Wilbur and Julie Lien-ying How. Cambridge, MA: Harvard University Press, 1989.

Education in Japan, by Richard Rubinger and Edward Beauchamp. New York: Garland Publishing, Inc., 1989.

Financial Politics in Contemporary Japan, by Frances Rosenbluth. Ithaca: Cornell University Press, 1989.

Suicidal Narrative in Modern Japan: The Case of Dazai Osamu, by Alan Wolfe. Princeton: Princeton University Press, 1990.

Thailand and the United States: Development, Security and Foreign Aid, by Robert Muscat. New York: Columbia University Press, 1990.

China's Crisis: Dilemmas of Reform and Prospects for Democracy, by Andrew J. Nathan. Columbia University Press, 1990.

Anarchism and Chinese Political Culture, by Peter Zarrow. New York: Columbia University Press, 1991.

Race to the Swift: State and Finance in Korean Industrialization, by Jung-en Woo. New York: Columbia University Press, 1991.

Competitive Ties: Subcontracting in the Japanese Automotive Industry, by Michael Smitka. New York: Columbia University Press, 1991.

The Study of Change: Chemistry in China, 1840–1949, by James Reardon-Anderson. New York: Cambridge University Press, 1991.

Explaining Economic Policy Failure: Japan and the 1969–1971 International Monetary Crisis, by Robert Angel. New York: Columbia University Press, 1991.

Pacific Basin Industries in Distress: Structural Adjustment and Trade Policy in the Nine Industrialized Economies, edited by Hugh T. Patrick with Larry Meissner. New York: Columbia University Press, 1991.

Business Associations and the New Political Economy of Thailand: From Bureaucratic Polity to Liberal Corporatism, by Anek Laothamatas. Boulder, CO: Westview Press, 1991.

Constitutional Reform and the Future of the Republic of China, edited by Harvey J. Feldman. Armonk, NY: M. E. Sharpe, 1991.

Asia for the Asians: Japanese Advisors, Chinese Students, and the Quest for Modernization, 1895–1905, by Paula S. Harrell. Stanford: Stanford University Press, forthcoming.

Driven by Growth: Political Change in the Asia-Pacific Region, edited by James W. Morley. Armonk, NY: M. E. Sharpe, forthcoming.

Schoolhouse Politicians: Locality and State during the Chinese Republic, by Helen Chauncey. Honolulu: University of Hawaii Press, forthcoming.

Social Mobility in Contemporary Japan, by Hiroshi Ishida. Stanford: Stanford University Press, forthcoming.

Pollution, Politics and Foreign Investment in Taiwan: The Lukang Rebellion, by James Reardon-Anderson. Armonk, NY: M. E. Sharpe, forthcoming.

Managing Indonesia: The Modern Political Economy, by John Bresnan. New York: Columbia University Press, forthcoming.

Tokyo's Marketplace: Custom and Trade in the Tsukiji Wholesale Fish Market, by Theodore C. Bestor. Stanford: Stanford University Press, forthcoming.

Nishiwaki Junzaburo: The Poetry and Poetics of a Modernist Master, by Hosea Hirata. Princeton University Press, forthcoming.

In the Shadow of the Father: The Writings of Kōda Aya (1904–1990), by Alan Tansman. New Haven: Yale University Press, forthcoming.

Land Ownership under Colonial Rule: Korea's Japanese Experience, 1900–1925, by Edwin H. Gragert. Honolulu: University of Hawaii Press, forthcoming.

About the Author

Anne E. Imamura holds a doctorate in sociology from Columbia University. Her first period of field study in Japan was in 1967, when she participated in the Junior Year Program of the East West Center, University of Hawaii. Since then she has returned often to Japan, lecturing at Sophia University in Tokyo and twice as a Fulbright scholar. Her interest in urban Japanese housewives began in 1970, when she lived in a small apartment overlooking a public housing project, a *danchi,* in a Tokyo suburb. Professor Imamura has also lived and worked in Malaysia and Africa. In addition to her work on Japanese housewives, she has published articles on the subjects of women and international marriage in Nigeria and Japan. Formerly on the faculty of the department of sociology at the University of Maryland, she is currently chair of Asian studies at the Foreign Service Institute of the United States Department of State.

▦ Production Notes

This book was designed by Roger Eggers. Composition and paging were done on the Quadex Composing System and typesetting on the Compugraphic 8400 by the design and production staff of University of Hawaii Press.

The text and display typeface is Sabon.

Offset presswork and binding were done by Vail-Ballou Press, Inc. Text paper is Writers R Offset, basis 50.